MIRARI

Also by Mari Perron

A Course of Love

The Given Self

Creation of the New

Love, Book 1 of The Grace Trilogy
with Julianne Carver, and Mary Kathryn Love

Peace, Book 3 of The Grace Trilogy

Mirari:

The Way of the Marys

From *A COURSE OF LOVE*'s First Receiver
MARI PERRON
A Dialogue on Mary of Nazareth's Way of Mary

Copyright © 2020 by Mari Perron.
All rights reserved.
First Edition, 2020

No part of this book may be reproduced in any form or by any means, electronic or mechanical, including photocopying, recording, or by any information storage and retrieval system, without permission in writing from the publisher.

Course of Love Publications
432 Rehnberg Place
St. Paul, MN 55118
Library of Congress Cataloguing-in-Publication Data
Perron, Mari.
Mirari: The Way of the Marys

ISBN: 978-0-9728668-6-6
Spirituality, The Feminine
Cover design by Terry Widner

All quotations are from *A Course of Love* (ACOL) unless otherwise noted. A Reference Guide to *A Course of Love* is provided at the end of the book.

Dedication

To you, the reader …
may you view yourself kindly, and me too.
Such loving kindness awakens us to one another.
Together,
from the heart of ourselves,
we may heal the heart of the World.

M

Contents

Invocation	9
Introduction	11
Anchoring the New	13
The Advent of Being	23
Lineage	27
Life in the Body	31
The New and Its Coming	33
Unknown Knowing	35
Transcending Love	39
Being in It	43
Joining in Resonance	47
Disorientation	53
The Matter of Holiness	57
Male and Female	59
What is Valuable?	63
Beyond Compare	65
The Eye of The New	69
The Surround and the Embrace of Power	73
The Purpose of The New	75
Feast of the Epiphany—"Here"	77
The Dialogue of Mary	79
Migration	83
The Hush of Love	85
The Womb	89
Life Goes One	95

An Ensouled World	97
Sophia	101
To Ensoul The World	103
The Childhood of The New	105
The Birthing Consciousness of Time	109
Self–Love and Suffering	111
Anchoring the Passage Into a New Age	119
Earth Time Holds Love Incarnate	121
Love's Warmth and the Embrace	123
Rise	125
An Opening in Time	129
The Great Departure	133
Power and the Time to Act	137
Rest in Love	139
Being Rocked	143
Be Still and Know	149
The Sacred Heart	153
Mirroring an Ensouled World	157
Experience	159
Creation of A New Language	163
The Irreducibility of the Two Is the One	165
The Power of Creation	167
Reject Nothing	171
The Perfect Storm	175
The Quickening	179
The Quickening of Desire	183
Palm Sunday	185
The New Advent	189
"In the Beginning was the Word"	191

The Temple Days	195
True Beginnings–Women's Authority	197
Soul, Destiny, and The New Covenant	199
The Soul's Distinction	203
Betrayal and Redemption	205
The Mystery: Holy Thursday	207
Miracles and Mirari	211
The Beginning of the End	213
The Place You Are Destined To Be	215
Remembrance and the Matter of Change	219
Remembrance and Grief	221
Death	223
The Breath of Life	225
Mourn	227
Recognition	229
The Day of Silence	231
Easter Sunday	233
Revealed Order	237
The Underlying	241
The Nature of Life is Change	243
Forgetting	247
The Forerunners	249
The End of the Past	253
Pentecost	255
Creation	259
The Key	265
A New Age	269
The Marys	273
The Non-Patterning of The New	277

The Time of Mirari	281
Making Sacred Through Acts	287
Doing for Love What We Would Not Do	291
Mirari—the Wonder of the New Self	295
Being Without Borders	297
Manifestation	301
Devotion	305
The Pattern of Time	307
Support of The New	311
Eachness Replaces Thingness	315
Revival	319
The Quickened	323
To Forsake All Others	327
Prelude to Our Way of Mary: Acts	333
Rest	335
Benediction For The Reader	337
End Note	339
Postscript	343
Answers to my Prayers and Gratitude for my People	345
Referencing Guide	349

Invocation

The divine does not often choose their messengers from among the … "fine." Jesus, and now Mary, take in the walking wounded, the hard cases, the troubled hearts.

    For the healing of the heart.
    As we heal our hearts, we are healing the world.
    Blessed Mary came … to me and to us.
    She came "back" to us.
    She is one of us.
    She lived. She birthed. She hurt. She healed.
    She went all the way down before she rose.
    Then she came *back* to us, to be *for* us.
    For us and our counterpart Mother Earth.

M

2 0 2 0

We are close now, close to a time in which a new choice can make true living available here and now. This is the decade in which transformation proceeds, and the time in which the mother's heart enters to show the way to care of the living, and the end of what does not need to be.

This is the time of Mirari: The Way of the Marys.

M

Introduction

Mirari: The Way of the Marys continues the odyssey I embarked upon in my forties, which seem now like still innocent years, and myself so young. Following a call to "work for God," I received *A Course of Love* (ACOL) over a period of three years, beginning at the close of the 1990's and concluding at the start of the new century. ACOL's original publication coincided with the tragedy and change of 9/11.

Now, *Mirari: The Way of the Marys* is being released during the heartbreak and worldwide change of the COVID-19 pandemic *and* the international demonstrations for equality arising from the Black Lives Matter movement. This movement came into prominence in Minnesota (where I live) with the wrongful death of George Floyd.

I believe that works such as these arrive in the world at the precise time in which they are most needed. They have a destiny that is linked with our own and meet us when we are ready.

Mary of Nazareth and I first engaged in dialogue with the opening passage of this book, written in 2013. But I wasn't ready. I set it aside. It was too radical for me ... then. It is not too radical any longer.

I am sixty-five now and a grandmother. It is a significant difference. The world is different. And …

The future may depend on an uncompromising, and revolutionary response to love … *Mirari: The Way of the Marys*.

Anchoring the New

2018

What does it mean, my Mother, to be coming into the time of the way of Mary? To be standing in this interwoven space of old and new, in readiness of a new birth?

You ask of meaning, but this is not about meaning in the way you look at it. You seek a description of a new way, a new time, as if it is a future that is already written. It is a future waiting to be birthed. An imminent birth that you are feeling with all your mothering instincts and concern for the new babe, the jewel of humanity and Heaven. We spoke before as women gathered around a fire, and I asked you if you would protect the children from the wild dogs. Do you recall this?

Yes, of course. The image of it, if not the content. You told me to feed no more male egos.

M

2013

Now it is like Mother Earth. Lead you into yourself. Plant your own seeds in your own soil. You are the seed and the soil as is She. The She of humanity. Now plant what gives back to yourself as She begins to plant what gives back to Herself, her living body. She is responding. Listen to her Roar.

Listen for the silence to break through. There, in the silence, where you hear yourself is where you are connected.

Ah, here the Great Mother has been provided to meet every need. Here is your example as well as mine. She and I are one in being, the manifested, the incarnated, not to be put asunder. We, who meet the needs of living are joined with Her, the unrecognized deity. She, no less than us, here to bring new life.

The matter of depletion is the same. There is only so far you can go before you must save yourself.

Light is coming to the morning, just blue behind the trees for now at 6:19. Inside the house, I heard a sound like wind roaring. It is nowhere in evidence out here. It is sacred morning, I can feel it, the turning away from victimhood has sparked it. It is where Mother Earth and I stand together.

This is our power: to plant our own seeds in our own soil. It is now given over to primacy, as the male planting of seeds was before, the primary. Do not get this confused. Nurture the males as you would Henry,[1] as you must nurture Henry, but not as servant to the male need to plant his own seeds, especially not in you. You are implanted from the heavens, your birth giving life.

It is the mother's way. Many chances to change given. Then the roar of outrage and depletion. Like a wild dog that bites the hand that feeds him—this is the unconscious world.

This is the oddest conversation.

But necessary. The "dog" needs training, but there are not enough trainers in the world to train the dogs. There will never

---

[1] My grandson who lived with my husband and I in the first years of his life (along with his mom) and returned to our care occasionally.

be. And so, the hand that feeds the wild dog must do so no more. Feed the meek.

Maybe wild dog is the wrong image. Somehow the poor dog got wild.

Yes, I hear your protests. But the wild dogs are in position to take over the world. They have, in many ways, done so. They would devour the babe. Participate no more in feeding the dog that will ravish the newly born. Feed no more male egos, no matter how uncomfortable it is for you to withdraw this support. "Let me teach you" is an ego companion.

Everyone "tries" in ways that please themselves. Do not let this "trying" fool you. It is not that there are not many wild female dogs. It is only that the victimless Mother is rising, and you are to be among those risen.

Imagine yourself in a village, a small village living on the soil (soul) of the Great Mother, many new babes among you. Will you let your small village be victim to the wild dogs? Would you leave them offerings outside your circle? Honor them as wild dogs? Perhaps. This is not a gentle time coming but a time to be fierce. Not to protect your "resources" but to protect the new babe being born so that it doesn't fall victim to carnage.

It is not stamina but wakefulness I call you to. Think no more of depletion. That is the old way. You rarely cease to call this radical "energy." There is "energy" that comes of no longer being a victim. There are new resources.

The sky is whitening before my eyes. A golden glow rising and the blueness of the sky ebbing like a wave going out to sea.

I know you can tell I am not particularly thrilled to hear these words, my Mother. I do not know what to do with this "as within, so without" feeling. I don't even know why I am putting it that way. I desire creativity more than this. I think you know that. And yet I do not really doubt that you are unleashing me from my chain, the last vestiges of my own wild dog ways. I can even sense that the "cared for" feeling I so desire will not come without this—as Mother Earth desires to be "cared for" as well as she cares. I finally withdrew the hand that fed one biting dog in my life, but now I cannot reconcile the dog with the person I see in therapy. So, your call to wakefulness? It is daunting. I fear I am like this still, at least a little: honest here, awake here, not so wakeful "out there." I do not desire this test, this burden, and yet I do, and I know you know this, too.

You need not call me "mother" unless you so choose. We are in solidarity, in the new "feminism" as you put it. There are many loving others "protecting their own" but this is not enough in itself. It cannot be done without, but it needs to extend. This extension is what you are beginning simply by being who you are, and the more you are who you are in your own life, in your own microcosm of biting dogs and as protector of the lovely Henry, the more you will be ready to extend beyond your current borders.

The whiteness now has extended around her borders. Two geese fly over, honking. Yes, I know they ask me to look out for them too. I appreciate this reframing of my small life concerns into the larger ones, and I will appreciate your aid today and onwards.

The new face of feminism, shedding our victimhood for the sake of the grandchildren and Mother Earth. Whatever it is, help me to be at my creative best for it. Let it come creatively, brilliantly, without trying. Let it flow if this is in your power, in the power of your own creative field.

My field is your field. This is what I am helping you to see.

We are together now to save this world so that Heaven on Earth can come to be.

M

2018

And as you have with the words of my son, you have pondered these words, as if on a back burner of time, and did not let them invade you. Some words are an invasion, a taking over, meant to seize you in your tracks, stop you, start you, cause you to move with new vigor and valor.

Only now are they in you in this way, a taking over.

My son, your brother, spoke to you of an in-between time, of the twin circles of one way passing and a new way coming into being.[2] Yes, my son is still my son, the son of God and the son of Woman, holy and human in origin and nature, attached to the earth and to all that grows within. The "within" is the incubator of all that can come to be, the womb of the imaginal realm, of all that exists "between" Heaven and Earth, held separately and out of reach. The reach is within. It begins in a mother's heart. It is a yearning for Life.

My mother heart was the beginning before the beginning. The beginning of a life with God in human form, myself only a young girl, yet to be honed by divine love. Too innocent to be skeptical. An unjaded innocent of good mind and a sense of possibility that I felt like the scent of a sweet dipped wind, moistening all that was dry. I was mystified by it all. Not in my right mind, barely in my

---

2 In *A Course of Love* (ACOL) these circles represent the way of Jesus and the way of Mary. See "intertwined circles," D:Day19.16.

body, but called back and back to body to birth the new babe. This is why I call you now—not as a young woman of child-bearing age, but as a woman in relationship with my son and with companions strong and true.

We are different faces of the divine, but we "were" human, and of the earth, and still are. We are with you in a real way and will accompany you on this next quest for what stands beyond meaning as eternal truth. Eternal truth brought low and sitting with the women and their babes born into The New.

My son spoke of anchoring The New,[3] and I want you to imagine now the women around the campfire, squatting while they tend the fire, squatting as they birth new life. This is the posture of the anchor, solid as an anvil, feet planted, balance fine and deliberate, poised. Poised for what will be needed next. Poised and ready for the invasion of The New and the old's lingering encroachment, as mesmerizing as the flames of the fire that signals The New. The invasion is an intrusion of The New into the old, a force meant to quicken the passing of all that lingers of death in the living. To end living death and welcome living life. To end division and become one with what is being birthed. To mother The New into existence.

Making the heart of Mother love, that natural duad[4] to the Father love that has reigned, brings the rising of the feminine and the balancing, at long last, of the masculine. Mother love has infiltrated the heart of the Creator God as an equal in creatorship,

---

3 "Others of you will follow your hearts to a bypassing of the final stage of the old and to anchoring the new within the web of reality." See ACOL Dialogues, D:Day18.1

4 A "duad," according to my 1998 *Third College Edition of Webster's New World Dictionary*, is "two together."

the Mother/daughter of the divine. This "life-giving" force has grown from the union of opposites and begins the dematerializing of opposites.

My power is belief in the miracle and in relationship with the Divine One. It is to be "our" power. It was as a woman that I was asked to birth the living Holy One in union with God. This is the way of Mary I come to bring to you—you who, along with your sisters and brothers in Christ—do not believe you know your hearts, or miracles, or God, or your life-giving power. This life-giving power is of the masculine and feminine "combined," of their joining, in love, in union and relationship. The physical need of male and female, joining to create a new life, is symbolic of the joining of the masculine and feminine into the wholeness that creates The New—new life within the realm that burst into being when the Divine One began to feel, through participation—the human experience.

The Divine One knew physical love with me, in all its sensation and intimacy; knew for the first time the joining of the human and divine. Knowing the joining of the human and divine enriched the being of the Divine One who had not before known of it, nor experienced maleness, nor femaleness—both of which the One was given in relationship with me. It was with me that the One first participated in actuality with his creations and directly created the physical in the God Man who was "our" son.

Yes, each life ever come into existence proceeded from the One, but not in this way that changed the Divine One's own being, for through me and our son, he knew human love in its fullness, and I knew divine love in its fullness without the consequence of death. This was the beginning.

This was the beginning of the "living" Holy One. There in secret. There, in the imaginal realm, secret love beyond the human mind's capacity to imagine and make real, birthed the truly real. There, Yeshua came in secret, a secret known only to those who sensed, in vague but insistent ways of the imagination, that into the world was coming something New.

Thus, began the birth of those who could see, and those who could not see. Those who could see needed no belief. Those who could not see could choose to believe or not believe. But only those who could truly see, knew Yeshua truly. This was not a matter of fault or grace, but of relationship. Life without awareness of the living Holy One is a failure of awareness of relationship from love to love.

Love to love has always made divine.

But there, in love outside of time, did time and eternity first meld into a potential for the evolution of humanity and the elevation of the self of form. Love outside of time is the way of Mary and the way of the birth of The New.

M

Do not let this take you over. This must come in the way of dialogue. You are to be part of it. My son and I have heard your anguish and we include you here, along with us, in relationship with us, to reveal your true heart. Do not seek again to remove yourself, for as you have seen, this is not the way of The New.

This is the way the great "they" of the physical world would have it be. They live by removing themselves. They desire for all to be so removed from the divine that they are comfortable with *their own removal. They preach the removal. We will preach the invasion, the seed of new life, what can be neither run from nor removed.*

M

The Advent of Being

AUGUST 2018

Yes, begotten one, there is another place. This is a question you do not know how to frame. It is like the change from day to night or night to day. We are speaking now of the advent of being, the waiting on the light, but in a different way—in relationship. This "reception" you do with "us" is in relationship, as is your relationship to the rising sun. Even when you cannot look directly at the sun's orange glare as it tops the horizon, you stay for it, and experience it without staring into it. You feel the sun's reflection, you see the change that comes to the earth, and as the "rising" continues, there comes a time when the light does not feel blinding. You know it and sense it, and feeling it, turn your eyes toward the sun again, and then it is over, and night has turned to day. And then it happens again, on the next day and the next.

You do not have to stare into the sun to know the light. Yet each day you await it. The coming of light. And then, not too long afterwards, the coming of dark. A cycle that is also a cycle of rest and waking. Jesus spoke of awareness of this cycle of the sun as the "art of thought,"[5] early in his relationship with you, and later he spoke of it as union and relationship. Oneness and relationship. This is the idea that, when you begin to want to speak of it, you do not know how to approach. It is accentuated by dialogue. Dialogues are demonstrations of oneness and relationship. That you are recording

---

5 See The Treatises of ACOL, Treatise 1, Chapter 2

these ideas that come into greater fullness as you and I relate, does not mean that we are relating in separation, but in union. Union does not negate relationship, or the way of dialogue.

Yet you are wondering about when Jesus asked you to cease your conversations with him so that you could realize oneness with yourself and all more deeply, and wondering specifically about this form of communication that comes to "you" specifically, and is meant for you and for all. You wonder why it comes as it does; why your own voice is supplemented in this way that speaks of what you are coming to know with, let us say, a larger view. But it is not only for the larger view. It is implicitly an invitation to relationship with the holy through the invocation and the address of Jesus and those closest to him, those who also had a human role in revealing the hidden truth. It is increasingly important once again, as the time nears, once again, for the coming of Christ. For the coming of "the truth."

Now, one of the reasons that I have had little to say through the ages, especially to those who revere the leaving of the body, is that I am Mother of the "body" of Christ. And I am deeply with you in the cause to bring "the body" into the realm of the living. I know of the importance of what some consider "small things" to be, things about care of the body, and the feelings of those who make this sometimes-desperate journey through life. I have known human life as both Heaven and Earth, and more specifically as the potential for Heaven on Earth, a potential now being actualized in the imaginal realm. While all is "one," there is within the oneness of Heaven and Earth, Heaven and Earth—and now in much more equal measure than in the past—the Imaginal. Preparation is underway for oneness of form and content.

It begins in the imaginal and extends into form through actions such as your own, that of many others, and the alignment of time and eternity in the cosmos.

My voice does not negate yours. My being does not negate yours. No more than yours does mine. This is also a demonstration. Heaven does not negate Earth, nor Earth Heaven, and neither the Imaginal—except as concepts held within the mind believed to be in the possession of the separate one, its intellect, the "source" of its knowledge, being, and personality. To become aware of this false perception is not to give up life in form, but to live it truly. Without some momentary awareness, true living is impossible.

The anticipation for true life, for the possibility of life being truly lived, has arrived. What this entails is still unknown, and so is being made known to those with eyes to see and ears to hear and with hearts open to relationship.

M

INEAGE

This word, *lineage* came to me and so I share it as a question to you.

 I will speak to you of lineage as the underlying, that which is both the Cause and that which underlies the Cause. It is that which connects. It is that which is of the heart—the pulse, the heartbeat of the world—and that which is in each. That which is beyond the known world, and that which is the hush of stillness that reveals the pulse.

 Yes, there is a "line," a connection between those who know the truth. It is through their extension that the line continues unto this day. It is a line of love, of mother love, of adoring love, of complete love that sees incompletion not. This line holds love's nature in suspension, a mantle ready to be draped upon every waiting shoulder. As your Jesus said, "Take on the mantle of your new identity. Your new Self." Those ready to "take on" cannot go out to find and grasp this mantle for themselves but are to allow love to bestow this mantle of the true Self. This is bestowed by those associated with the lineage of the Marys, those unafraid of revival of all that is true despite the authority of those who have proclaimed themselves holders of the truth.

 Let the attraction to this line be a sign to you and take no imitations of it as the truth of it. This mantle does not reveal but conceals. It protects the living Holy Ones until the moment for which they have prepared arises. It is given those who gather in *preparation of The New. Ah, to be bringers of The New. In this the heart rejoices.*

M

Blessed One,

It is the next day, Sunday August 19, and I have sat reviewing about a week of my journal, finding the words I wrote that sparked my question regarding lineage. Here they are: "The lineage of light. The coming of light. And the blind can see."

Oh yes, it is a lineage of light, a light in which the blind can see. Remember my telling you—those with eyes to see knew who Jesus was—those without eyes to see saw him as an ordinary man. "The light" speaks of those who see. This is the lineage of light. Let this help you to realize what you already know. It was important that you see the way in which the question first arose in you before I spoke more of it. Let this expand your confidence in your knowing.

All light is of love. Love is the light in which the truth is seen—not as fact—but as reality.

Darkness is that from which the sun rises. It is a good metaphor for the coming of the son of God, one easily grasped. But light is also truth, and not only as metaphor. It is the light in which distinctions, such as that of religion, fall away, and a simplicity—a minimum of words, expressions, and feelings—are needed. Some need only the light in which to see, and not the seen or the seeing. Others, those of the new way Jesus has given through you and Helen Schucman,[6] are given to see the light in each other, in Holy

---

6 Scribe of *A Course in Miracles*

Relationship, in union and relationship. This too is our lineage. It is a lineage of those who treasure the seen. Those who see the manifestation of the Holy in form. And especially those who, with laws of the Mother, discount no "one." Those who discount not the tender needs of comfort, nor the need of food or drink, healing and consolation, Earth and home, giggling and weeping.

Human evolution has now come to a place where all needs could be met. Before this capacity was reached, humankind was still closer to the plight of the animals, whose needs are met through survival instincts. For humankind to pass out of this survival instinct, the Mother laws of care and nurture—given to all—must come into their time of fullness. This is part of what can create a new age and make way for The New.

The imaginal realm, which you might consider one that exists between life lived from survival instinct, (which is the life of those grown callous and greedy as much as of those who act from desperation) and life lived in holiness (the babes, the afflicted innocents, and those ready for love without fear), in the in between. The imaginal exists, in the between, to preserve sacred "living." All are holy in the light of love. Yet those who have darkened their hearts, have grown into the capacity to make life unlivable. To make life extinct. This may happen in time but not in eternity. This is for which we prepare, for the entrance of time into eternity, and eternity into time: the continuation of the living Holy Ones, birthed into The New.

This realm called "imaginal" has existed for ages, and is assonant to the heartbeat of the world, its freedom, and its protection. You might say it is the world's mantle. It exists, a reverberation through the ages, and not a prediction of an end, but of the con-

tinuity, the lineage, if you will, of the living Holy Ones. Holy harmony.

(*Your life in the cave,[7] in which your bodily needs shut down, and where your life once ended, was one of years—not days, as was that of Miriam of Magdala. You knew this imaginal realm, which my son reminded you of with one word, a word that has called to you through the years and that you now have stopped to consider in earnest.*)

M

---

[7] Experienced as a past life during a healing that occurred in the time of receiving of ACOL

Life in the Body

In my time, life lived in the body was a fulltime occupation. Could I forget my son's need for water? My particular duty (as well as desire) to care for his body? To care also for my own so that I did not leave him? I was not arrogant about myself or God and watched for arrogance in my son as he grew. I did not want him revealed too early, before he was ready. Even while the time of his revelation was not up to me, and this I knew, protection from speculation and the range and breath of humankind's unkind envy and assumptions was part of "me" as God's eyes and ears and heart, and most particularly arms and hands through which care was given. As what you did with your hands was not a skill of typing, your typing was not immaterial, your hands and heart, as mine, were given to be in service of the One whose love we are.

I did not know to what extent Jesus was aware of who he was as he grew, and I knew it was not for me to tell him. No one told me this, but I knew, just as you know, without being told, of certain essential things. Some knowings are not those dictated by nature or divinity, but by our own soul and circumstance combined. These knowings can have to do with the practical of human life and yet are still knowings of the wholeness and balance of time and eternity ... in the particular. Your knowing. My knowing. A knowing like instinct only stronger and surer and more specific. Knowings that sometimes are fleeting—coming in a moment without thought—and that at other times are of a long-range nature, a knowing of the way that is unfolding in time.

Every "knowing" is God-given, so there is no need to distinguish from "where" knowings come, but the ways in which they come are many and varied as they encompass the whole of life. Most of what is known today is not actual knowing, but rather "knowledge of." Much of what one has "knowledge of" is not knowing at all. "Knowledge of," being taken as "knowing," is a major correction that A Course of Love and the way of Jesus are making so that our way of Mary can anchor the remaining transition. This is the wholeness come of combining the feminine and masculine in each. It is the precursor to the combining, in awareness and actuality, of the human and divine.

In everyone there is a—not "appointed"—but more of an "appropriate" time for them to come into their fullness, a time that depends on this awareness without arrogance, and without overwhelming neediness. This is like the time that you have faced since Jesus came to you, and it is faced by each. It is the call of wholeness that has to do with the challenge and the change of life in form.

Ah, Mother of All, thank you. And Mary, I hope you are in delight over the happy birds feeding outside my window. [8]

You are in me; I am in you. We enjoy together. We reverberate.

𝓜

---

8 I often "ground" myself in this way of looking out the window.

The New and Its Coming

Dear Holy One,

Since you "know" me, I know you are aware that I have felt a pause in my creative writing. I had hoped, on this sabbatical, that it would return to me, and I believe it hasn't so that this relationship with you could come. It doesn't really matter, but it is almost as if I feel I must be honest, forthright about my missing of it. "This" is another way of creation which I honor and respect tremendously and was pleased to have Jesus speak of as my way.

My expression of the words orally falls into disarray if I haven't got written words before me. I am not concerned about this, and I am happy with this gift, but at times it finds me briefly comparing and wishing that I were more eloquent in my speech.

Ah, begotten one, I know that in your holy relationship with my son, you felt a shift in your being and your dreams of "who" you would be. I see that in this long time of coming into your new being you have struggled "in relationship" many times and mourned your creativity many times. You have also had experiences of tremendous growth and a brave and honest way of communicating that which is not easy to express. In ways unknown to you, but known to us, you have experienced the advancements and the setbacks that are common to all. "All." Different forms, different specifics, but nonetheless common ways of transformation in time outside of time—in time. This is not an easy landscape to navigate and is why such help as this is being offered.

You have wondered, more basically, if your claim of "I am not perfect" hides imperfections you choose to keep. And I say to you, keep what you will. This is not the time for focus on changes to the immaterial. You are the right person, in the right place, at the right time—which is spoken in the imperfect language of your time for a reason: it works. This is not about niceties now. Not about politeness. This is about, at the most basic level, the awareness that The New is coming and its anticipation. This you knew and sensed before I spoke a word of it. So many more are also aware, and so many more than these are to become aware. And awareness creates. Awareness creates a new reality.

You sensed this and began bringing it forward in your talk in Philadelphia. "We are in the time of the second coming of Christ." You are an announcer of this coming, a herald sounding the horn, lighting the fire that will anchor The New. You have found a voice.

Thank you, Holy Mother.

M

Unknown Knowing

It is funny, Holy Mother, that you have said I found "a voice." I think the voice I have found is yours. And I've thought, 'Of course. As you were there for the first coming, you will guide in the second.' I have taken a middle of the day nap because I could not keep my eyes open—literally. I have now returned to the cabin[9] at 7 pm, with a deja'vu feeling of arriving at seven this morning. The shadows are now on the opposite side of the yard, reminding me how seldom I sit here at this time of night.

I have been imagining how some might rage at me for the questions I don't ask, and there is a funny thing about this that continues from my time with Jesus. When the opportunity to ask questions arises, they are not forthcoming. I get senses of things in the same way I had the feeling of not being able to keep my eyes open. I slept for a while I'm sure, but I was likely in bed several hours in between sleep and waking. That I "literally" could not keep my eyes open has translated into a question I don't know how to ask.

Ah, my daughter, you are suited for this work! This work coming out of your time of "inaction." This giving and receiving that you have been invited to, and have entered, is a way that makes you look out at your evening-lit trees with morning wonder. As you spent hours in between sleep and waking, what you experi-

---

9 After *A Course of Love* was complete, I had a great yearning for solitude. Over a period of several years, in miraculous ways, the opportunity to purchase the woods behind our yard, and for my husband Donny Deeb to build me a cabin there, came to be. I call it my "Course of Love" miracle.

enced was like unto your time here, and to your time of becoming accustomed to the way that—between sleep and waking—there is a somewhat muddled awareness, a registering of time outside of time.

Dreams have often been the silent couriers of The New.

You awaken from a dreamless, intermittent sleep and return to the cabin to be with me, recognizing a receptive time when it is with you. You recognize when time is with you in a way "other than" that of ordinary time. You have long been thus and are well practiced in this ancient art that so few recognize. You yourself have not recognized it until this moment. Now you can see it as having been with you throughout the time of your life, acknowledged in certain heightened periods that called you to be present for them.

As you said that, the neighbor cat walked down the path, as if announcing the presence of "another" here with me. It is so still that without the wandering cat, and one bee that approached a budded weed, time might be seen to have stopped entirely, despite the buzzing, swishing sound of the traffic. I have never "seen" my trees standing so still.

You have also long known (in your unknowing way) that "time" includes an infrequency, a "freeing" of time from its compressed nature. It is as if time "compacted" becomes unstuck and of itself elongates. New waves pulse outward like the beating of a new heart. This is the time in which we stand together.

Not knowing what you know, is, in essence the way of The New. When the unknown becomes the known, the solidity forms, and so in The New, what is known will be known in this fluid way, a pulsing in and out that will keep it free from being structured into knowledge "of."

The quiet trees are speaking over the voice of the noisy freeway. Yes, you are understanding . . . without knowing what you understand. Can you accept this?

I believe that, as you say, I have been doing so for some time, and even, in recent years, given up the search for knowledge "of" what I know.

Yes, I bless you for this acknowledgment as it is essential to The New that you not "grasp" for knowledge.

I do not believe I will, and with your help I am nearly, very nearly, almost "clearly" certain . . . that I can refrain from doing so.

Well, there is nothing in the way of knowledge "to know." There is a dismantling of knowledge in this time of coming to know newly.

Still, nothing, absolutely nothing moves.

There you are. Here we are. Together in the still point. And now, looking out your window, you begin to wonder if you are seeing drizzle as you did this morning. There seems a nearly invisible presence to the air that stands between you and each bush and tree.

Yes!

This is not drizzle but presence. The gift of what stands aside from movement, being, and expression—and the gift that allows true movement, being and expression—also allows true stillness. It invites movement back in a new way, a way that transforms your passage through the world and these final days and years of your living. It has begun thus and will continue thus. The old and the young are those whose awareness, without any training whatsoever, will begin to assert itself in the way of unknown knowing. Both stages of life are innocent of the middle, and you are held here in such a time of innocence: the innocence and the intimacy of unknown knowing.

Now the noise sounds noisier than ever before.

Your sensitivity to noise will be benign even while it heightens. "Noise" is like the crashing of sound waves. You will continue to be sensitive and you will begin to hear a new sound more akin to a lack of sound. The waves that have been crashing will begin to still for you, as your trees have stood in stillness all this hour.

Out of the metaphor of time standing still, out of the silencing of the movement of time, will come The New. This is what the anchoresses knew.

The new anchoresses will stand between the stillness and the noise as between the darkness and the light.

M

Transcending Love

Holy One,

You will know that since I left here, I have become—I search for a proper word—almost undone by a joy that feels too grand "for me" and yet speaks with great hope for humanity. It came of you having called me "Begotten One," which I did not think of as it came. Only last night, when I returned to my reading on Mary Magdalene, was I reminded of "begotten not made" and the difference which I can't at all express but that I know speaks to the sort of humanity that Jesus embodied, the ability to retain unity while in form, the heart's connection with its Source. That is the best I can say it.

Then a little farther in my reading, before I had recovered from "begotten one" was the word "reverberate," which you used in a closing to me, saying "we" *reverberate*. I know that I am receiving so much more than I am aware of receiving! And I thank you for allowing this reading to happen so that I am aware of the "more" that is occurring here, the truth, the sacredness, the way your knowing is coming into me, even before I understand its import. There is a link, in this shared wisdom from Cynthia Bourgeault,[10] between reverberation and the begotten.

I can't express it! But I am so happy for these spoken human words, while at the same time, they are too much for me in a way that I realize that you and Jesus are not. You are "too much" in another way, a way of my heart's feel of you and your essence and

---

10 *The Meaning of Mary Magdalene*, pp. 194-197, Shambhala Boulder, 2010

truth, but not in this way of words that, while I am happy to have them, so happy, and know that they furthered me in my belief—catapulted me really into total belief in what we're doing— are not "for me," for reason of them being *too much!* I simply cannot take them in without thinking. Regardless, they came to me "for this reason" of strengthening my belief in what is being revealed *from our union.*

I am now more totally yours than before, and as certain that you brought this reading and its ability to raise me beyond belief for this reason, and for, I suspect, an acknowledgment of my participation that will not allow me to negate myself. Even while my instinct is to try, something in me knows. This time . . . I cannot do so. I am "in" something too holy for me to stand back and say, "It does not include me," which is what all my yearning has been for, to accept that this, and that your son's words too, have included and transformed me, even while I remain with these human imperfections that you thankfully say matter not.

Thank you so for bringing this reading to me at the perfect time, for setting me on the perfect page, for this show of abundance, and of the way the divine works.

Yes, Begotten One, you have taken in something that you do not understand and will not understand, not for the purpose of keeping you mute or stumbling, but for the purpose of The New, and the "pure singleness of knowing." Each must come to this knowing from within their union with themselves. The new knowing engenders, more than anything, a trust in yourself that is paramount to the coming of The New. Without trust in one's own knowing, no matter how oblique or unspeakable, there will not be this advent of The New.

What you are asked to do is to build anticipation for it, not to explain it. The feeling that a new time is here is pervasive, even in those who have not recognized it at all. It is there, but unrecognized as what it is. So much is like this! So much that is like this will remain knowledge of if explanations and truths, meanings and inner knowing, seem to be the same.

If you were to continue your reading, you would find many examples of the very odd, disturbing, and inexplicable signs that reveal The New. Why? Because each must discover for themselves, take the journey into the realm beyond what has been known, encountering the unknown in intimacy.

I know you have further questions of intimacy that have the feel about them of disloyalty. When you feel you can be intimate with one and not another, even one considered a good friend, you are troubled. This is not a matter of love or fidelity or strength of friendship. This is a matter of resonance. It is like a harmonizing that cannot take place between two singers of a certain combination—and that cannot fail to take place with two others of a certain combination. There is a particularity, an alchemy, specific combinations that, in coming together, create what can be created in no other way. You have known, deeply known this with Mary Love,[11] and what you feel is beyond loyalty ... so far beyond. It is a knowing of, as you have spoken of it recently, a destiny field."And it is a knowing that this field is beyond your choice alone. You cannot determine it. It is not up to you. And it is very much up to you. These are the combinations that leave the logical mind reeling.

---

11 Mary Love and I "knew" each other on meeting over 25 years ago and have been spirit sisters, creative partners, and co-authors of *The Grace Trilogy*.

In the case of Mary Love, the timing, while you once viewed it as long delayed, was perfect as you grew together. With others you sense that such resonance will never be and yet do not want to admit it, some for cause of associations already entered, others for care of not hurting one's feelings. I know this is difficult in some areas yet, for you. It may continue to be.

Do not be afraid of this. This is not an area in which to be overly sensitive or to doubt yourself. You "know," oh so newly, "that" you know this field. This is a divine marriage, when one forsakes all others, all who are not of the same field, the same resonance, the same heartbeat, the unified reverberation. Not in a manner of exclusion, but in a manner of choice for unity and The New, for the beautiful music, for the fullness of truth, for the promise of revelation.

Other bands of resonance will keep the old in place until The New is birthed. Some bands of resonance will die out before too long. The time has come for this intimate knowing. The hunger for it is more vast than you can possibly realize. Rejoice that you are aware of its magnificence and know that as it is seen it will grow. Like a bee to a flower, the innate being of each will be seen to offer exactly what it offers, (no less, no more) and such couplings will abound in the elevation of the form of The New. Each will find the One within God's creation who will join to them in resonance and thereby open them to the universal in this exceptionally personal and loving way. Thus, will love be remembered in this time of the Second Coming of Christ ... in the imaginal realm.

M

Being in It

SEPTEMBER 2018

We are in a new month, Holy Mother. September. There is something exceptional about it suddenly, this new month, one that I have dreaded in my lack of belief that I can hold time and energy differently. I have noticed a difference.

Yes, Begotten One, you have! I spoke of the "form of The New"—of the difference "of the form" of The New, and you noticed. I love making you happy in this way! It is the same, very nearly, to the way you view your beloved woods when you do not have your glasses on. The scene is not so different, but it is different. It is softer, and the blendings are greater. You can still remember the "distinction" that suddenly came to your then equally beloved Cherokee Park, when you first got contact lenses. Your trees had been like a faded or indistinct picture and suddenly they were marvelously complex, not a blur but a field of a thousand leaves—separate and distinct.

Now we are blurring once again, softening, blending. The "form of The New" will be new. Your body and its softening are a bit like this as well. You think you do not look like yourself and have at times given this to weight gained. Yes, this is part of it, but only part. You are softening, blurring, blending.

It is like unto getting the idea of a right to live; the right to live freely. To be given— "given" the means to live so that one can choose to share their gifts and not only work for a living. Working to live is enslavement. And so, the world has become a frantic place. You can picture the slaves building the pyramids. As seen from above, they would be like ants. The ants still abound. Your freeway noise is the noise of the ants, the drone, the whine, the frantic pace that does not know to stop. As you have not known to stop. Only in your stopping have you had the room to feel my call. You suspected it was there but could not feel it, and in not feeling it, did not know it. I thank you for your attention to me as I know you thank me for attention to you.

Once a work such as this begins, as with your Course, there is a cessation of the sense of being called and a feeling of being "in it." You and I, "we" are in relationship now . . . as you were and continue to be, with your Jesus (whom I called Yeshua in life and will now continue to speak of in this way, which is more natural to me). As you have seen, the togetherness does not end. "We" share the view of your squirrels and the blur of trees seen without the aid of your glasses. "We are each other's own." We are not separate but blended, and so the call to see the blending, the softening, of form; a literal softening as what you see without the aid of perfect sight. What you see is clearly different now than what you saw before you removed your glasses. It is the most perfect of examples, coming at the perfect time.

When life is not so hard there is a softening, and this is what you have felt for having removed yourself from the hardness of a busy life. A busy life only works if it is structured. And as you began to be unable to "structure," to structure "yourself" around your busyness, you had two responses: one of worry and one of relief. You knew deeply that it was time to quit forcing yourself, and it was and is "the force" of structure within time, that does the *deepest harm to tender beings, both those totally unaware, and those on the verge of The New.*

The hardness of a busy life is not only of time structured into heavy bricks but systematized into "a" structure. It is not precisely the arrangement of time as viewed on a clock, but it is the structure of time bricked into foundations as strong as castle keeps. Time is a rampart. A fixed point made solid and unyielding. A menace. A captivity around the daughters and sons of God.

The image with which we began years ago, of the women around the circle of fire, had no ramparts in its vision. And yet it was not unprotected. The women, dedicated to new life, knew not of any structure around The New. Their attention was devoted to The New, symbolized by the children in their keep, and the wild dogs outside their keep—the wild dogs spoken of—but not in evidence.

Women and children grow depleted in the most subtle and most brutal ways. Powerful men now, as with the men of ancient times, bow to selfishness and strengthen their self-proclaimed "right minded" use of their power to dominate. Men of power now, in great majority, fall to the same demons as those in the past, and often women of power join them in their will to dominate. And so, it is the perceived power of this time, just as it was the perceived power of our time, that creates the divisions that in their totality "construct" the old and reinforce it.

"The old" is a construction. What is constructed can be de-constructed, and it is in this time, that those perceived to be powerless will rise and begin to claim "unconstructed" power, the innate power of the feminine that exists in all. It is available to be

cultivated in any willingness to step outside of the "constructed" ways of old.

The constructed is that which tells you what is real and what it is to live in the constructed "reality." And, it is that which tells you what it is that will befall you if you step outside of the "protection" of its structure.

The will to dominate is also the will to divide. Without the structured reality there would not be easy lines of right and wrong, master and slave, and the shield of righteousness would be easily pierced by any eye not too blind to see.

This constructed reality does not call for revolution in time, but for the revolutionary transformation of time outside of time. This is what your Jesus called you to share and to experience, and to grow into. So many lives are growing in this direction now! But many, not knowing it is a new way of being—a way that calls them out of the construction of time—simply build new and softer looking ramparts in which they feel greater safety and well-being.

Yet safety lies not there. Safety lies in expansion of The New, in transcending love relationships that create, with the effortless fluidity of the imaginal realm, and there beget The New.

M

Joining in Resonance

Holy Mother, thank you for our wonderful morning together yesterday, and for my acceptance of a restful afternoon unstructured by time. Can we speak more of transcending love relationships and their link to the imaginal realm?

Begotten one, you feel reticent to bring to me that of "your own life," and yet there is a relationship, your relationship to Mary Love, that is like those you have known as Jesus and Mary Magdalene. I bring you back to your earliest offerings to one another. She suggested that you write "your story," the story of the three,[12] and you asked for her to share her journal writings on the life and death of her daughter, Grace.

Mary trusted you enough to bring her secret writing forward. Later, you set yourself aside to bring her "Grace writing" to the attention of your publisher, feeling as you did, that it held something so pure that it surpassed your own. You imagined that on seeing this writing, it could possibly be chosen over yours, and you accepted this potential "sacrifice" of your dream for what was—and this is essential for you to understand—not only your friend, but the purity of truth at the heart of her. This was the trust of Holy Relationship that you felt called to by Jesus' words in A Course in Miracles. *This purity of heart, that came in the rela-*

---

12 Mary Love, Julieanne Carver, and I, began our spiritual journey when working together at the University of Minnesota, and called each other "spirit sisters." See The Grace Trilogy.

tionship between herself and her daughter Grace,[13] *became in this way, a connection not only between you, but with those beyond space and time.*

Thus, were two human beings given over to the imaginal realm, even while you knew it not.

This is what you are coming to know about the imaginal realm. It is of relationship and the creation that ensues of "the two" gathered together by the heart of the truly real—the true reality. The true reality of the human being is one that exists "between;" between time and eternity; between one and another. In its "living" it encompasses both. You had entered this realm we call "imaginal" with Peace, an angel of light. You had known "of" this realm with Jesus, but not "entered it" for two reasons: the abstinence from direct contact suggested by your faith, and for awe translated into fear of worthiness.

Yet in this selfless giving to one you knew as soon as you met her, you entered living relationship with another human being. And this is the "way" of the way of Mary. The way of "the Marys." The way of union, human One to human One is the creation of the human Holy Two. The joining of two as One, and the parallel joining of the two phases of time and eternity, occur as one in form.

My son used the word "imaginal" to draw you to recognize this way of living that you had already encountered and yet were struggling with, particularly during the formation of the Course given to you. In a sense, this formation split your loyalty. You remained overly awed by your calling and its manifestation and confused over what it meant "for you." You entered a time of at-

---

13 Mary Love's daughter, Grace Zuri Love, died when she was five weeks old.

tempting to make yourself *"self-less"* rather than *"self-full,"* and this caused your struggle for return.

Now you are ready to be self *"full."* This feels possible when you are with Mary, less possible when you are apart from her.

M

To accept a shared *"destiny field"* is not always an easy agreement, especially when it is *"known,"* but not fully believed for not being fully understood. It can be taken as a loss of independence rather than a gain of unity. It has nothing to do with dependence or independence but with a joining of equals in resonance. This resonance, when spoken from the heart, or heart to heart, is adoration.

Adoration is personal, person to person, person to Creator, Creator to person. It occurs *"between"* one and another. This *"field"* that is *"between one and another"* (not in separation but in union), this field that joins one to another in love and adoration as well as truth, is, in time, *"the imaginal"* and is, in eternity, Heaven. Heaven on Earth will grow from the imaginal realm, from its warmth and care and love—not from knowledge *"of"* such a place, but from the actuality of it and its explosive ways of creation: Creation of the New.

I remember that in *A Course of Love,* Jesus said that your way represented incarnation through relationship, and would "demonstrate the truth of union, the birth of form, and the ascension of the body."[14]

You could not have received more and could not have shared

---

14 See ACOL Dialogue, Day:17.10

more on the way of Mary without the realizations that were to come, not only for you, but for many. These years have made a difference—as you have seen. The primacy of the thinking mind is giving way. The heart's cognition is finding acceptance. The pomposity of powerful male egos has become too blatant to be ignored. Women's voices are rising. Now is the time for us, for the incarnational, for the birth. Now is the time for the imaginal. Now is the time for the realization that all of what has happened to birth the great religious and spiritual traditions could not, and did not happen without women, and did not, could not happen, without the establishment of the in-between realm—the imaginal realm. All of the recorded history of the divine happened "in" the imaginal realm.

What was brought forth, even from this realm, by thinkers and as "teachings," by those who "knew of" but did not know, was not adequate. This led to what was institutionalized and has only inched awareness along. It is why the two Courses of Jesus were brought into time after the Nag Hammadi discoveries, the records of those who "knew" rather than "knew of," and has to do with the elevation of "the knowing" of The New. This is about the way in which The New is "known." The shift to the "knowing" itself is the fruit of the heart and of Heaven. It is also the shift away from the institutionalization and corruption in the structure of those devoted to "knowledge of."

All truth that passes into time from beyond time, is incarnational. In this way, many men have given birth already—to the embodiment "of truth"—rather than to a new person in truth. Jesus is the only person known as the "embodiment" of truth called the "son of God." Even while he shares this designation, his particular designation is called the hypostatic union, and is spoken of as the union of the Trinity in the "person" of Jesus Christ, the "wholly human" and the "wholly divine." This statement of union refers to bringing the essential nature into form. This is one of the few areas in which truth found its way into "translations" of truth, even if in a limited fashion. In this realm it applies to the above and the below.

M

What I have just shared has included some areas of "information as knowledge" in order to contrast now, the way in which we started, with my description of the sweet love, the physical love that created our beloved Christ Jesus. Was it real or unreal? How can one imagine God in the act of procreation? And I can tell you that this is what I felt and knew, through "feeling," to be the truth, and accept as truth, and pass on as truth.

I was raised to believe in much that was not available to be known "from the outside," and also to be pure of heart and thought, so that contaminants of what you call ego would not reside in me. There is no need for you to believe me, but I am suggesting that this is a demonstration of the new "form of the form," of the truth. What is more real? What I, as a woman, experienced? Or what was decided to be the truth? And why does it matter if it was only the truth "to me," or that you have truths that are only the truth to you? Does it matter? Or does it not? What matters? What ... is the truth?

M

Disorientation

Dearest Holy Mary,

I have been gone awhile, investing myself in the affairs of an on-line conference because the sweetest man, James Kelly,[15] asked me to. His idea was to celebrate the beginning of *A Course of Love*. But now he must tell people "what they will get out of it" and has me thinking of incentives to offer them. As we got into this side of things, I became sick to my stomach, and realized since then how disoriented I am.

There is a disorientation that comes of receiving in this way, this engagement with you. It is as though nothing is what it was before. These last days of interacting with him reminded me of the time of receiving *A Course of Love* and how I felt with what went on then. There was this plane of existence on which those I met with resided, and there, their mouths moved as they spoke their words, and I was somewhere else, on another plane, where none of it made any sense. I can still feel myself, sitting there in that living room nineteen years ago, *feeling* that. It was returned to me. I did not think I was so far "into this" that I could have such a feeling. In comparison to the way it was with *A Course of Love*, we are going very slowly. And yet I cannot deny what I felt.

Disorientation, begotten one, is having no fixed point. Our time together is what makes that fixed point recede. The fixed

---

[15] James Kelly, who hails from Ireland, discovered *A Course in Miracles* in the mid-nineties and more recently *A Course of Love*. He created the Miracle Choice Game (ACIM).

point is, in one way, the "reality" where your dear James must tell people what they will get out of it, and in another, the place where those who must be told, "sit," as, in the time of the Course there was the living room in which you sat with those you are remembering. You were there but unable to feel that fixed point that "being there" was for those you joined. A fixed point is your reference point, what you "refer back to" without realizing that you are doing so. It "places" you in a certain "point," at a certain time, in a certain story. You had been taken out of your certain story.

By adulthood, almost everyone lives within a certain story. It is who they are.

A soldier at war, an astronaut—they lose their fixed point. A person lost in the desert is the best example. It was a real possibility in my time. It was the birth of many mystics. To be removed from your fixed point is a blessing.

A traveler experiences this when she steps into a vastly different environment. But the traveler can seek adjustment and re-orient herself quickly—within days if not hours. Yet it still has benefit if the person feeling so can "experience it," rather than approach it as a problem to be solved. Your disorientation is not a problem to be solved, and you do know this.

You are experiencing disorientation, and this way of expressing it never occurred to you in your time with the Course. "Orientation" also refers to the rising of the sun—or the Son. The word refers also to the stars that guide, that were literally the guides of ancient time. They "oriented" the traveler, on land as on the waters. The "disorientation" of time gives way to orientation, which you feel as disorientation.

M

Origin has the same root as orientation.

You sit each morning, oriented toward the East, watching the sun rise. Here, you are with my Son and with me and all the blessed ones of life in time and beyond time. Place yourself in that orientation to the rising sun if the disorientation gets too great. This loss of the fixed point is a step forward, but disorientation is disorientation. You feel the loss of your fixed point as a disorientation with the orientation that is the way of this time in which you live, the way of such things as conferences. The towns and the marketplaces of my time were similarly disorienting. You are wise to have fellow travelers with you, as were we, when we ventured forth. Know that this disorientation will happen and be prepared, as we were prepared. We did not travel alone.

You are traveling now in a new way.

Does this have anything to do at all with our last dialogue, in which you began to speak of truth?

Surely, I say to you that it does. Disorientation was your experience, in one sense, the truth of it. But behind the truth of what you felt was the Cause of what you felt. Many losses of this time are the gain of truth, felt and delivered by the Source. For the ultimate Truth, you travel always back to the Source and Cause of Truth. You leave your fixed point to travel thus.

M

The Matter of Holiness

OCTOBER 2018

I am associated with being pure. How, the Fathers of the Church wondered, could Jesus be born to a woman with the stain of sin on her heart? And so, they "made me" holy, but could not quite commit to it. This behavior has continued.

There are still those who wish for some to be holy and for some to not be holy. I say to you, be watchful of those who proclaim either sin or sanctity. Not wary, but watchful. Notice them when they are about you. Notice when this assignment finds its way to you. Be particularly watchful of language that carries this idea forward. Join with your Mary Love in creating a new language of the heart ... of wholeness. What is whole does not judge, nor is it deceived.

There is a difference between judgment and the watchful eye that is not deceived.

Having been deceived, once, twice, a thousand times causes, most often—doubt about oneself. This is the most insidious result the purposefully deceptive can hope for. Fewer than you think are purposefully deceptive. It is simply the nature of the divided to deceive.

Unconsciously, when attempting to blend with a "whole" that is seen as the place in which safety and love is sought—from first forays into schools, to national politics—it is the same. One secures their place in the "whole" of their known world in this way, and then begin to "protect their own."

M

You have "entered" wholeness to do this work of bringing the truth that exists in "time outside of time," into time. This is one fluid action as you relate and receive in our dialogue. It can become another action when you must relate and receive "in the world of time" as you bring about manifestation. This is where your disorientation most often occurs. Being aware of it can cause distress and is a reason that we are continuing with our help regarding what is, at first, a "new" way of knowing.

Most of those who will begin to experience this way that is "not of the world of time," will experience this disorientation. It will not feel natural. Even though it is the natural knowing of the daughters and sons of the Divine Living One, the disorientation can cause retreat. "Retreat" might be considered a natural response rather than a failing or a delay. By this I do not mean a retreat from the Truth, but a retreat from the world in which the Truth has not, as yet, been acknowledged and accorded the spaciousness in which it will come to be fully accepted in time.

You, who are creating The New, are creating the spaciousness.

Your retreat, (your time "apart" from the structured columns of time) is a natural inclination that allows for the anchoring of spaciousness, of openings in the constrictive world of time.

M

Male and Female

Let us speak of the male and female dynamic that is troubling you, and that troubles many women in almost unspeakable ways. The masculine, "male" dynamic, is a sense of authority and a right to it, as if it is their due. And particularly with women—many women, including you—you sense it, feel it, hear it, but do not know how to respond other than by shutting down. In this shutting down one of two things happen. A placating offered by the woman that is taken as "the right" of the masculine-leaning person who receives it, or a shutting down within the woman or feminine person, wherein she/he avoids response.

There is something like a shock that occurs to the sensitive one. This is why the reaction often comes later and then one feels it is too late for a response. There is the feeling of "the volunteer" who contributes out of the goodness of her heart, but who has no authority. Women do not need to be volunteers to feel in this position. Authority, to the feminine-leaning person, does not feel to be a "natural right" as it does to the masculine-leaning person. It is simply not thought of.

The feminine leans toward receptivity, which is an open, sympathetic way of being. The masculine leans toward a confident and authoritative way of being, one due respect. The masculine is convincing by nature, and sure that to accept what is offered is a *favor and a means of support.* To "hold" and "share" is a feminine quality. To "share" and "hold" is a masculine quality.

So you can see in your own dynamic of feminine receptivity that you hold what you have received to your heart in love and belonging—it is your own, it remains your own, cherished and held within you, part of you. And yet you offer it, share it, with others—from your own being.

The masculine tendency is to share what they have received of another in a way that appears magnanimous, and may even be magnanimous, while they also "hold on" in their practical, hands-on way. The very fact that they do not hold it to themselves in their sharing makes it seem a freer offering, even when it is shared as a commodity (whether of form or knowledge) on which they retain a hold. This "hold" is where they derive their authority, and it is an external holding ground. It is not of their own being even if it is their own original idea or creation. They will "make something of it."

The feminine will offer to share "what it is." To "share" is not to give away and place it outside of oneself as an object or thought, but to share most naturally through the inner warmth of what they hold.

Feminine sharing is direct (even when it does not seem so). Masculine sharing is indirect (while it appears direct). Direct sharing starts from within. Indirect sharing begins with an outward orientation. Feminine sharing is inward and intimate. Masculine sharing is outward and protective. Together there is provision and responsiveness. When in conflict, there the masculine will assume the upper hand. This is often due to the delayed response of the feminine one who goes inward for what she gives, goes inward for what she shares. She feels an allegiance to what she holds within. As you discovered as you wrote Creation of the New,[16] "the one who merges the inwardness and the outwardness, who combines the inner and the outer, does not leave her soul in a pot on a shelf."

"You are being prepared for spiritual motherhood"—which you heard from your Jesus years ago—did not mean that you would give birth and send your creation into the world unloved and untended, or that you would direct its life, or its interaction and growth in the world. But that you hold it in love and rally to keep this "child" from being turned into something other than what it is innately? Absolutely. This is a natural and optimum response.

M

---

16 A mystical vision put to words. See *Creation of the New*.

 hat is Valuable?

Dearest Holy Mother,

I have been away again, still enveloped in the long-awaited opportunity to share who I am, both through the online conference and a new website. Due to these two things I have been crazy busy but seeing much that is "new," particularly in my ability to be in joy while working collaboratively, and to recover more quickly when I get overwhelmed by the "intensity of sharing." It is not "work" in the way of old. It *is* an intensity of sharing. That is why (along with your support—the support of all of those in time outside of time) I can feel miserably overwhelmed and wake up recovered, or even get a second wind in the evening of a long day. It is confidence building.

I can also see more clearly, why "the old" holds no appeal. "I" was not supported or affirmed. "The work" was. Even by me. I see my part in it *and*, I am beginning to make the turn, finally, from "the work" element of it all, to the primacy of sharing and creating. I can see that it was my own former lack of acknowledgment of the need for it, that was so draining. Oh, Mother, I feel your presence and yet do not have much time this morning. Yet I can make time. I am so happy about that! I can, with you, make time outside of time as the sun shines its light on the trees that were, only minutes ago, in darkness.

There is an intensity in sharing, as you say, a magnification as you experience with Mary Love. This is, in truth, the magnification that is her greatest gift, and which you missed so much when you were absent from it. But you also possess an enormous passion for sharing which will come out more and more as you find those who are also capable of creating, in equality and intimacy, from who they are. There is no "thing" to share, which is the upside-down thinking of the world.

There is Bob Dylan sharing who he is—that is the essence—not the recording. The recording is the manifestation of the man, (not his work) and is why some true artists occasionally rise to fame in the world. The "intense sharing" that comes of being true to one's self is recognized in the art, if not at its source. It is hard on each (popularized) one, to remain who they are, and to continue to give as who they are, when their work, their inspiration, is commoditized. It is difficult as well to continue to intensely share when there is no one, or only few, who recognize what is going on—the bringing out of the truth of what is within—which is also the adding of spaciousness to the world.

This new "information age" has the potential to democratize the process, but there is still a lack of recognition of what is "true." What is valuable. And as the floodgates of information open, this situation will not be solved. And so, it is up to those such as yourself, to do just what you are doing, and to emphasize the intense sharing as the golden, gentle, power that it is. The "light" that it is.

M

Beyond Compare

NOVEMBER 2018

It is snowing! A beautiful large-flaked snow, coming in at a slant from the north, heading east. I am sitting with my eastern orientation, and it is calling me to you, Holy Mother. As I am sure you know, I have been getting myself a little riled up again wanting to protect, or keep others from misrepresenting, *A Course of Love*.

The snow is swirling now, and I wonder if you share this experience through my eyes, or in another way.

It is "who we are" that is shared and accorded acknowledgment. I know "with you," and you know "with me."

The sharing is an offering that, in the response, becomes a dialogue. In dialogue, each can share the same bread, the same wine, the same story, the same plot of ground ... but in different ways.

Yet there can be no comparison. No one can know another's experience in the same way, which is the sanctity of the One whom we each are.

Dear one, it is a much more intimate knowing, but there is a sanctity to each one, as there is to the Divine One from whom creation sprang. We each know the way of creation that we participate in, in what you would call a "personal" way that is "beyond compare." As your trees acknowledge you, and you them, there is communing, a shared knowing, but it is "beyond compare." The way I share with you is the same.

This is the idea in "A Treatise on the Personal Self," isn't it, Holy

Mother? The idea that we remain endlessly who we are? I remember when I read my first angel book, one of the Emmanuel books, and this angel, Emmanuel said just that ... that you remain endlessly who you are. I found it to be an awful feeling. I always had thought death would release me from who I was and especially who I had been. I thought of it as a sentence to carry guilt and shame through eternity. But I guess, in a way, it did make me begin to see "life" as the place of healing, of redemption.

Redemption restores by fulfilling the promise of life. And the promise of life is that you will return, return to the Self the Divine One created, that original, pristine, wholly, and perfectly created Self that you are. This unbounded love of the Creator is like the eye of the hurricane, the dot in the circle of the spacious Self, the Source and the activity that is the refinement of the new life that is "yours."

This is where the idea of separation came from as well. In this way that you were created, what is signified—in every way possible—is the sanctity of the One, which is you as well as God.

The sanctity of the One, "is" you as well as God.

It is the ultimate freedom or the ultimate bondage—to have a life that is beyond compare—to have a life no one can live for you. The difference between attempting to live "for" another and to share life "with" another, is the difference that the Beloved One who gave us life ensured through our creation as we are. The Divine One has been enriched by having returned to him, those not given a chance for life. The gift of life is really the "chance" of life in each one, the possibility of knowing the freedom of The One in the Many, the true freedom of union and relationship.

M

Those called to our way of Mary, know of this freedom in, you might say, an inner way that anchors, and an outer way that nurtures. It is a way of holding and of letting go at once . . . giving and receiving as one. It is directed, through personal peace, toward a peace in the world that is achieved through peace in each one. It is not a passive peace but a life-centric peace that protects, most of all, the life of the soul, and the fulfillment of the soul's purpose in you.

This "protective" energy is what you might see as the difference in our way of Mary, and it is essential for this time in which The New is destined to be born. While the way of Jesus stirs those toward The New, the way of "the Mother" is to nurture the new life that arrives there with equal parts freedom and protection. It is as if the world and all its people become the child who is being brought to maturity in the loving arms, the embrace of our protection. Some will be nurturing the many, and some only one, and it is all the same. Our way calls for firmness as well as gentleness, and equal compassion for those with whom we must be steady in protecting against, as for those we shield until their lights can shine brightly on the world.

Do not forget the image of the women joined around the fire, and their position as both anchoresses and protectors.

Let this fire among you, and this fire going out from you, guide your way.

M

The Eye of The New

DECEMBER 2018

You called me to be with you this morning, Holy Mary. "You" wanted to talk to me, rather than as it usually is, "me" wanting to talk to you. Even when I do not say it or ask for it, I usually *feel* it, which today I did not. The conference has just ended, and I am still adjusting into the "new" that now is. Today, it had little outward sense to it until, rather than stop everything to speak to you, I heard from Steve[17] and then Mary Love, both of whom are excited about the momentum. I like hearing that word even though I can see and feel no momentum at this time.

I was ... surprised. There has been so little response! It is hard not to get response.

And now I see that, as I wrote in my journal, you said, "Let us proceed into the way of Mary. It will soothe you." That sounds so good and yet almost discordant with my sense of something like impatience.

M

I say "soothe" because you are afire with ideas and wondering which way to go. Let us talk of your direction as we move forward from this eye of The New.

Let me repeat what was said when last we spoke: "Our way calls for firmness as well as gentleness, and equal compassion for

---

17 Steve Wiebe, a friend and website coordinator

those with whom we must be steady in protecting against, as for those we shield until their lights can shine brightly on the world."

You have had a way of being both easy-going and intense that you have seen with some idea of letting it go. You have seen it as "going along" at times. You have seen it as "catering to" at times. You have seen it as pacifying, or as fighting.

These ways you have seen things no longer fit you or this time.

You can have compassion for those you must protect against. True compassion. Not placating. Those you must protect against do not recognize The New, but many of these same are where they are to support you, even though they do not understand that they are. They think they are in place to support "the Course." They do not see the union of you and the Course, and this has pained you and caused you to want to leave them behind. But to leave them behind without changing the status of who shapes the coming time would be less than protective.

And so, I come today to assure you that your protective instincts are needed. What you are protecting is the emergence of The New. This is crucial. There are those in waiting to "grasp" The New and bring it forward as their offering, in their way. They can really do no harm other than delaying The New, but the delay is a harm. Without the growth of The New, there could be a return to an even more staunch protection of the old. This is a natural instinct of those who feel they are in possession of truth and know the way. You simply know that the new way is not "known" in the old way.

Therefore, it is essential that you have a voice and use it; that you have power and that you let that power be known. Do not shy away from these ideas that are filling you now. Embrace them.

Take your power. This is the way in which you are to be fierce for The New. Take up your power.

Yes, I feel that I know what you are talking about Holy Mary. Thank you for your reassurance, and guide me and my voice, and my companions.

With all my power I will do so, as will your brother.

M

The Surround and the Embrace of Power

But Holy Mother, what if my power lies *here*?

Of course, it lies here, my daughter, in the endless equality of mothers and daughters, as of fathers and sons. For many young men and women the father is all wise, and then as maturity comes to the sons and daughters, the father will seem to know less, the mother more, and the same is true in each area where maturity arises and people live absolutely beautiful, honoring, heroic, valuable and loving lives.

Each person in the world is the new babe born in innocence and coming to maturity within the surroundings in which they do, which seems to be their life. You often see your life in review: on Smith Avenue, at the University, as a single parent and so on. That was "your life." Those were your "surroundings." Your sense of place was always keen and so the scenes of your life play out in "place" as much as with people. Even when you do not see it as such, there is much that is vivid and alive in these memories . . . some sweet, as those of childhood, some uplifting as those with your Mary Love, and many nearly devastating, as those with men or with experiences of guilt over your own behaviors.

This is the way each one views life.

But "here" you at times escape this view and all you knew of "that" life. You set it aside. That is what "here" does. It sets the old surroundings aside for the new surroundings.

I know that you are feeling how perfect is the word "surround." We speak not of the meaning that is to "enclose" but of the meaning that is to embrace. The New surrounds like the embrace of gentle waves, lush fields, both earthly and divine.

My heart is pounding with the feel of this "truth."

Yes, my child. Yes. Let yourself be both innocent child—held and protected—and brave woman, fierce and protective for The New being birthed.

Thank you and my husband for this "here" time in the cabin with day fully on the rise at 9:00 exactly!

M

The Purpose of The New

Dearest Holy Mother,

I am "here" this morning, but also "not here." You know my concerns about the shape of things with the future of ACOL, and that I cannot escape them. Can you let me know if, when this happens, I am meant to simply be responsive to those concerns, or if I am to bring them here?

M

Dear One, only days ago you wrote: "I am here now for the purpose of The New. No other purpose."

This can be your guide, and you are being shown continually the crucial nature of this dedication. You are in a more difficult position than many, being a "light worker" who has the work of manifestation in your stars.

You have spoken of celestial relations recently, and I would like to use the word "celestial" to suggest such a vastness that does not invite the forming of a central idea. Some will say that an idea as outrageously amorphous as "The New" needs to be brought together into a recognizable image and further named, as have been the stars; one aspect of The New distinguished from another aspect of The New. Soon, the different aspects are contrasted, and there is a new philosophy. This is the tricky part of The New. The "forming" can't be prevented, and so soon, the crucial idea is darkened, and the twinkly lights of the "next new" begin to beacon.

This is due to the shaping instincts of the human person, who, in this foreign land, feels in need of structure and defining lines, and is uncomfortable staying with the "burst" of The New, the continual "here-ness" of it, and so begins to arrange it into thought, and the thought into new "forms."

Even you will be prone to it. Even these words will seem, very shortly, in future "time," to be fixed in "a" time, the passion of a certain "sect" in a certain period, the same way the "living word" of my time became the basis for many forms of a new testament, then one accepted form, and finally, inevitably, a divisive rather than a unifying form. There has always been a desire to either suppress or utilize The New. This is where the trouble begins.

M

Feast of the Epiphany— "Here"

JANUARY 6, 2019

You have laughed at yourself for never having been fond of the idea expressed as "Be Here Now."[18] But then the emphasis was on the "Now," rather than the "Here." So let us continue with the idea of "here" that you have felt so long as you sit at your cabin window.

The meaning of "here" is "this one." Her ... or him. This "person." "Here" is not just a moment in time, but the "experienced" moment. The "experienced" moment is the person experiencing it, who in experiencing it is creating it, and casting newly the stars in the heavens.

I love this, Holy Mary. It gives me hope.

You are here in this time and this place to "create" The New, which means that you must experience newly, not think new thoughts. This is the difference in the emergence of The New. The crux of the difficulty in the emergence of The New is the ideal of thinking new thoughts.

This is the point at which many "leave the world," leave their structured life and begin to practice meditation and any other methods that will break them from their thoughts. You participate in this practice in this way, the way of letting your thoughts go for the reception of words coming to you from time outside of

---

18 Coined by Ram Dass.

time. This is your way of creating The New, right here, right now. Not in the future except for those who, from reading the words will also receive them and experience moments of time outside of time—in time. This is our chosen way of speaking of what is happening, the diminution of time's constriction and the expansion of spaciousness.

When you envision Heaven, you envision this spaciousness. It has been so from the beginning of time. A dream of spaciousness. Life without form. Life in the clouds. A dreamy vision of no structure, no obstacles, no concerns, no thoughts like unto the old.

All of you are stuck in thoughts about your thoughts in a world of structured thoughts: thoughts given form. This is what we do not want to continue to help facilitate: more thinking. Do you believe that your divine Brother gave you the words of your new Course so that you would have more to think about? No! The idea is to make thought over in the way of love.

I applaud you for coming back here in your times of thinking too much. Here is the way of creation needed and ready to become the new mode of your loving ways of expression. When you get "out of your thoughts" you calm down. "Here" you are able to receive words that arise without thinking. This is possible in all areas of life, not only the "here" of your cabin, while at the same time, the "here" of your cabin becomes an expansive space in the world. It is a place of miracles.

M

The Dialogue of Mary

Dear Holy Mary, I hope looking out at the cabin keeps me in miracle-mindedness, which I did not pray for yet today, but pray for now. I hope the sunroom is a place of miracles, too. Would you like to continue?

M

Now we are ready, daughter, sister, self, to begin in earnest the dialogue of Mary, the way of the passing down of wisdom that has always been the way of the Holy Word. It is first delivered One-to-one.

Do your people of this time not see this? No! They do not! But this is not a complete impediment to them. As they accept "our words" as theirs, and hear "our words" as spoken to them, they begin to open to the One on One. This will find them in awe of beginning to hear for themselves, in the way of the Holy Word. This is crucial: To realize that one hears for herself or himself. It does not matter how the words come if each one "takes in" what they hear "for" themselves. When each "hear." When they hear before they think.

Listen, and you will hear these words in that way.

The way of the written word is exceptionally beneficial. But the origination of words is of what we speak. The one-to-one of the origination. This was spoken of in A Course of Love as thoughts you did not think.[19] *And so, it is in the intimacy of reading words, alone, in the space of one-to-one, that much knowing is gained by having been "taken in" by these "thoughts you did not think" in this one-to-one way. Does one need to understand?*

Did you, Mari, with A Course in Miracles*? No. You simply "took in," and in that taking in, did not separate. You held the words within yourself. Your instinct was not to stop and understand until the point at which you began to "hear," shortly before* A Course of Love *announced itself, that you would have a role as what was called a "teacher of God."*[20]

Only then did you begin to try to understand the words that had before rested within you, held close and dear.

This prophetic tradition of "the Marys" was "taken in" and "held." The prophets, male and female, did not often "understand" their prophecy. When they spoke it, it was due to a feeling of great necessity within, a necessity much like now, that was born of a "knowing" that the old way could not continue without crushing the spirit of the people.

In the way of Biblical times, the liberation was always brief. One need for deliverance followed another and another. It is still the way of time that is as ancient as are the women and men who have populated it. It is the way of time, which is why we now move to time outside of time. Time outside of time is not a way

---

19 D:Day3:39-40 and D:Day5.3

20 My friend, Lee Flynn is an ACIM scholar who is devoted to ACOL as well. He paraphrases the first two paragraphs, M1 and M2, of the Manual for Teachers, this way: The teacher's "qualifications consist solely in this; somehow, somewhere he has made a deliberate choice in which he did not see his interests as apart from someone else's." ... The teacher becomes "a bringer of salvation." ... "The Call is universal."

See ACIM's Manual for Teachers, *A Course in Miracles*, copyright 1992, 1999, 2007 by The Foundation for Inner Peace, Novato, CA.

or a belief. It is an actuality that can be lived now—in time. This is the way of Mary, the way that is now being revealed, created, and anchored in the "reality" of time.

The "reality" of time is what was created and made real by precisely the endless search for liberation of the human spirit from the human being enslaved to the meeting of the needs of the human form. The Marys, in their tender attention to human form "and" spirit, met these needs with provision that was "care," more so than protection. Male protection was the field of the liberators called by God to "movement" ... to move the people out of bondage, to move the established authorities of oppression off their thrones, to move with commandments of love.

The movement sought to reorder the field of time so that the people, nurtured by the care of the women, could know their being, their soul, and their liberation—both as individuals—and as part of a greater whole. With their keen sense of the spirit being ever present, the women facilitated the birth of the God man who would take movement, being and expression[21] in a new direction, combining love and liberation in the knowing of a field outside of time.

The "words" of the Marys were expressions of love, very personal, quiet, and intimately shared one to another. Their expression of their longed-for freedom was done together, in song and dance that literally opened space. Compassionate care and attendance were offered, beside often grueling work, to the living Holy One who would combine movement, being and expression.

The Holy One was held with great receptivity within, and vig-

---

21 See D:16.1 [M]ovement, being, and expression come together into the recreation of wholeness that will be expressed in the elevated Self of form.

ilant attention without, manifesting the first combinings of the within and the without. The words your Jesus gave you, "I will keep your vigil. Now keep mine,"[22] speak to each one of the devotion needed to enliven all who have not yet known what it is to join the movement, being, and expression that will bring The New into being. This will happen in time outside of time.

We will speak of "movement, being, and expression" together, as "mobility," as being mobile: available to be moved, affected, changed. Available to migration. Available to versatility, to change, to The New. "Available" is a step beyond willingness. It is a willingness to show up, to be in and "within" the movement to The New and to do so as the being and expression of The New. To, in mobility, gather in The New as one would reap the yield of a ripe field; to gather in The New as to come together in the realm of The New; and to gather the ways of The New together so that the hope of the people can initiate creation of The New from all quarters.

M

---

22 See The Jesus Chronicles @mariperron.com

Migration

This is not to be the upward mobility of an elite, but the making of the mobility, the migration that is change for all. It is the way of the prophetic tradition of both the male and female prophets of all time: a move from there—to here.

What is new is that which can hold, in this time, the from "there" to a new "here"—before only symbolized by geographical movements—and make them into movements to, and creation of, an internal geography in the field of time outside of time. It is the advance of knowing one another outside of the realm of location in time and space.

Ways of a common telepathy are one such movement, not new, as is evidenced by dynamic movements such as those having occurred in the 1960s, movements of young people tired of the old: Movements that burst out in France, in the United States, in Mexico, in Prague, in music, in protest of war, in calls for civil rights and women's rights. The readiness for change was a spark that was lit from within consciousness and felt around the world long before the first events took place.

This current movement will be greatly enhanced, even while it will be quiet, a whisper rather than a roar. It began, in this new period of change, with the translation and publication of ancient writings and the growth of diverse ways of spiritual thought and practice, combined with the adoration felt by the devoted of every religion.

The liberation movements of the young and disenfranchised, utilized all the commercial and practical methods available. The spiritual movement did much the same. Many new activists of this time will do so as well.

The way of the devoted religious women and men not held by dogma but by love, the way of those untaught and unschooled other than by their hearts, was and is, not a movement that relies on any outside source at all—but a continuation of adoring—a carrying on of the way of those of pure heart. Those whose adoration is of love, live not by the ways of the world or in the arms of the world's comfort, but in the way and arms of Who they have known to adore and give their hearts. They do this without thought of benefit, and with little interest in the mind's way of knowing.

These will be silent partners in The New, even if they do not know that they are part of it.

But those who "know" that they are of it fully, and meant for this new time, are called to nurture the recognition of the way of love and union, and the time of love and union coming together in time outside of time. It is a way that creates a new wholeness, a wholeness that fashions the consciousness of The New.

M

The Hush of Love

We are the heartbeat of the world.

The Hush of Love is that from which the world arose into sound and light. This was not the creation of the pregnant or the gestation of the babe in the womb surrounded by the heartbeat, the rush of blood through veins, the gastronomy of the body. Love in its conception was, and is, All. All that would arise out of the great silence.

(The hawk has just flown in, my Mother, and landed this time.)

And this is the first time you have called me "Mother" naturally, and without hesitation. And it is perfect because we are about to speak of the origin of the Mother.

This Hush of Love is that from which God the Father, the masculine, drew the first "thought" of Life. The feeling of love is of the Mother, Sophia, the feminine in the Creator who is known as God. The sound and light of Love is of the Mother, perhaps the reverse of what you might have thought, until you realize that the Creator who is known as Father is both masculine and feminine—as you term it now. It was Sophia, the feminine in the Father who, in that primordial Hush of Love, arose as feeling and thus birthed self-awareness— "thought and feeling"—one-to-another. Thought and feeling birthed the desire to create, and over time the desire for a "second."

I was chosen to create along with The Father, our Holy Son.

M

The prophets, and all those aware of love beyond this world prior to the God Head's joining with me, knew of God separately from the Being of God. They heard God's words and did His deeds, thus preparing for the second Hush of Love in which I came as Mother Love incarnated. To "us" came the babe who would truly bring light and sound to a world still devoid of the original light and sound of God, the heartbeat of the world: Love Itself. Born of us.

In us was God's loneliness first abated, and in our son was birthed the capacity for all to live with the awareness of God "in themselves."

This will be too touching for those of your world to accept, and yet it has arisen in myth repeatedly. Whether it is spoken of as myth or truth, it is that which, prior to science and in concert with science, fueled the imagination and creatorship of humankind to this day . . . this day in which the time is ripe for an acceptance of a new story: a story born of love.

We are the heartbeat of the world.

M

And "here" we are again, on a new day with the sun rising over your beloved slice of the world and the first of the squirrels on your plot of ground twitching their tails.

"Here" includes all of it—the mess as much as the glory.

You awaken to reflections on your life: the stings, the shocks, the tender disappointments that brought you "here." You. Here.

You, in the sanctity of your singularity, your "aloneness" in the world, your battles to accept your plight in life, your migrations. We speak in the way we do, not to form new thought but to paint new pictures. We speak in the way we do not to plot new maps but to stimulate vision—the vision of the heart. "Here" we carry this vision of the heart to the vision of our eyes. We join the listening ear with the seeing eye.

We refurbish the lens with which you "take in" the world and its happenings, the personal and universal. We negate neither. We rock with our Earth Mother's heartbeat. We know why we rock.

We rock to the heartbeat of the world, our "known" reality and its Source.

We drink of the well of spirit and we know God. We get a drink from the faucet and we know God. We. You and me. We forget all others, for all are one with us.

This is the call, the welcoming call to what is more than One, and relation from the more than One to the always One.

M

The Womb

Would you like to continue?

Yes, Holy Mother. My brother has told me that you will help me with what just occurred between us. An impregnation of spirit, felt in my body, in my womb.

M

From my journal:

I am here, my brother, and welcome you so, so much.

This is the beginning of your day when you are, as our mother says, "here." What do we, together, my sister, know to be real? I could say "love," and this would be true, but what is in greater evidence "here" is we know our sharing together is real. Yes, you are right to notice the "we" being used by our mother and myself. A greater "we" is being brought into being. A more direct "we." A "we" that you will begin to access more and more until it sustains you and is in you fully. The "I" of, "I need do nothing," becomes the "we" who create together.

I would like that, Jesus.

Then it will come to be. "Come to the mountain" as you heard from the "afar" of a sister on the other side of the planet. Come to Me, Come to the Mountain, Come to our Mother ... but "come to." Come to consciousness, as you come awake in the morning, as victims of trauma and near death "come to consciousness," returning to what animates form with spirit.

Okay. I will come willingly, brother, from my own spirit, not only because you have asked.

Blessed be, my sister! Blessed be! This is what I have been waiting to hear. You know, when you wait for me, I also wait for you. Let us be done with waiting now.

Yes. It has been a long awaiting. A long "coming on," of being fully "here."

And so, we begin again. We begin with "our" power. I will be your partner and help you with all you need to do and say to represent our Course in the world ... as I use your words: "the new we formed of you being you and me being me." We will do it "together." We are "in it" together now. "Here" together. I promise to support you with this partnership now that you are ready for me to do so. Your readiness is my permission.

Thank you so much my dear brother, for your respectful awaiting. I know what you say is true. I can feel it in my bones ... deep in the marrow of my physical being. Time feels as if it has stood still.

Yes. Here we go ...
Ok okokokokokokok
I feel a heaviness in my ... womb? ...

Yes. For men it is the gut. For women it is the womb. You are impregnated now with the Second Coming, which will not be for form but for spirit, but which will incubate in the womb. Our Mother will help you with this. Go to her now, and then be on your way out into the world ... newly.

Thank you for the wonder of this day, my brother.

M

Yes, my Holy Daughter, I will help you. This is relationship from the more than one to the always One. You are New on this tenth day of January in the year of our Lord 2019.

Birthed into twoness that is a gestation in the womb of the living Holy One, an implanting of seed for the harvest in time outside of time. Take care now of the babe within. This living Holy One who is now One with You.

We are one ... in truth?

One in truth, and one in a new reality of truth. You stand now in a new field.

I wish I felt a difference other than this pressure in my womb.

Do not be quick to wish the feeling gone and do not worry. Hold all within. This is the gestation.

I feel as if I could burst.

You will! You will burst into newness.

SPEAK IT OUT, SPEAK IT OUT, SPEAK IT OUT.
USE YOUR HOLY WORDS.

IT IS DONE. YOU HAVE AGREED TO BEING SUPPORTED. YOU STARTED THIS.

Yes, I know.
There is a life waiting to come out of you.
Yes, I know.
And now you doubt your readiness.
Yes. I know.
It is done.
Yes. I know.
There is New life waiting to come out of you.
Yes. I know.
AND you will be supported.

I look out on my yard, as if looking out fondly on a life that I will be giving up.

Yes. I know. I doubted too. But once you have agreed, it is done. And this I know. You have agreed. It will be good to get out now. Go out as my sister rather than as my daughter. Go out as one gathered in the hush of love and the quiet whispers of the women. This is not the masculine energy of going out to conquer the world. This is the birth of the new world. It is all held within. All you see is held within. Closer than you will ever be sitting at your window.

The scampering of your squirrels, the twitching of your cat's ear—all are held within and birthed anew. All you see is birthed anew along with you. Go out a while and bless all the world you see. And do not forget that you go with support, or that "you" are the greatest support you have now, because you are "new." This does not mean you are unsupported but that you are supported to the greatest extent you can be, because you are fully on board now, fully committed. You have agreed. Given your assent. Chosen and been chosen. Your support has come. It was always yours to give.

(After leaving my desk and preparing to "go out into the world," I realized I have not supported myself and looked into the mirror, into my eyes, and from my Christ or soul self said, "I support you." I felt my soul, as my incarnate self, gaze back at me. It was transformative. I did go into the world newly. I set out into my day and was saying, "I support you" silently to everyone all around. I had cute little conversations in Target. I came home happy!

I then spoke to Kate, who channeled in voice, and finally to Christina,[23] to find that we are each in the same place. It is almost as simple as we know what we want to do and what we don't want to do ... and they, too, recognized the need to accept being supported. A truly miraculous day!)

M

---

[23] Kate Macnamara reached out to me a few years ago after being touched by ACOL, particularly "The Embrace" (C:20) which was pivotal for me too. We talk regularly and she has visited me. Christina Strutt and I met in 2009 when we were both feeling drawn to solitude. We have been friends ever since, and she has given tremendous energy to the new way of *A Course of Love*.

Life Goes One

It was only this morning that I have gone back and read the chain of events of the past week. There has been a build-up, a build-up of something "coming" that I cannot honestly say I felt in the way I have in the past. Having reread, I can't believe I had a nearly normal day yesterday, as if I had forgotten what occurred. Not forgotten, but surely not in remembrance or with the sense of awe I now feel. It was likely a time of grounding—Henry here, normal things occupying me. But reading back? Reading the sequence of events? My womb again feels full to bursting and I am stunned on this Saturday morning, and may need to wait until later to join you "here" fully, as Henry is in bed still, and life goes one. Ha! LIFE GOES ONE. I like that! And I will go about my day, One and Supported, and silently greet those with whom I live with this support.

(Sunday 1/13/2019, the same has occurred. I have reviewed again and again my womb feels full.)

M

An Ensouled World

The joining of the physical and the spiritual in his new way will always be felt within the body. It can be a sign to those who come after you. Many are with you already, and many have begun as you began. What you are experiencing is landing in the field outside of time, within time. When this is spoken of: "anchoring time outside of time in the field of time," its meaning is first of anchoring time outside of time in "You." It is You who will then anchor your new Self, thus expanding the spacious way of time outside of time—into the cluttered way of time— "in" the time that has been.

I use your brother's word, "spacious" and it is enough as we continue, speaking of the spaciousness of Heaven brought to Earth. It is like unto a leaving of the planet. Although you are still "here," the "here" in which you still are has changed, and in this change to "here," what was is replaced with the spaciousness of Heaven and ... much more easily spoken of ... with the soul's life in you. The animation of form with spirit has now become the animation of form with soul. It is the irreplaceable creation of the signature heartbeat in each one, each one who has come to live her or his destiny in the world. We have just made room for an ensouled world.

You may envision your body as the world, and your womb as the birthplace of your soul.

This is the birth each will be asked to allow in the time of Mary.

Each one, living their own unique destiny, will ensoul the world, which is the softer way of saying, and imagining, the creation of time outside of time within time.

The soul's life is in you. It is she who is your support, the same support you have now accepted. It is she whose eyes return your gaze as you look in the mirror and say, "I support you."

It seems so simple, but it feels so good. What I say is, "I support my soul and my soul supports me." I have also added, "I support time and time supports me." I do both in the mirror before bed, and in other parts of the day.

It does seem too simple after all the buildup of thought and words that have led you to this time, doesn't it?

The simple is the most complex of all notions for the thinking mind to accept. The complex can tell you, if they are so inclined, each step in the forming of the human body, from sperm and egg to cell divisions; but they cannot tell you why those steps occur, or why they result in life. If they could, what would these steps answer for them? Would they know more of the living one? In what way would they know? In what way will soul be known to you who are now aware of whom you carry, of the life that enlivens you? Of the seed of the Mother/Father God that came not of sperm or egg but of the dynamic and migratory force of love.

A flock of geese flew low overhead just as you said that.

The geese celebrate along with you the ensoulment of the world they share with you, and now share newly.

M

As your geese "fly," Love "moves." Love moves into Being, whose life is given to express the living Holy One whose birth it alone can facilitate.

Will this birth produce a new Eden? This birth produces the movement to being and expressing this new Eden. Your soul is needed for this creation, for your soul, like unto those of us who know you, will create "your" Eden, an Eden that will infringe on no one else's Eden, an Eden that will, in freedom, embrace each one's autonomy and choice, and where, guided by soul, there will remain the complexities that some enjoy, and even the choice of suffering for some. For the soul is both you and God, both the "here" of this time and place, and the "here" of another time and place.

The birth of the soul is the bringing together of time and space ... in you. It is the coinciding birth and creation of your destiny field. Your destiny field is where you will meet those who, along with you, create the space for all choices of love ... and none other than choices of love.

M

ophia

Your "aloneness," your inner sanctuary, is the passing on of your inheritance from the Hush of Love out of which the Divine One's own consciousness of Being arose. Feeling, was born of Sophia's awareness of Being, and together these became the nature of the Life of Love, the sound and light, the creation, the third of the trinity that stands at the beginning.

This I tell you only to help you to see that, while Love was always present, awareness was not complete until both thought and feeling were birthed. This duad of thought, coupled with feeling, is what you now call the masculine and feminine, which only in relationship, could love, and create as Love creates.

Love has no attributes because it is the "before" from which attributes arose and moved always toward extending Love's creation. God was, and is, Love's awareness of Being via the relationship of thought and feeling. Awareness (as of thought alone), the thought of "I Am" was not enough. The feeling of "I Am," was the completion. The masculine and feminine of "Being in union," is that through which life extended as Itself.

The thought and feeling of Love are the light and sound of the world.

Now we move on from the past to the present and to creation of The New, to creating as the God "Head" (masculine) and the

God "Heart" (feminine), to creating with the thought of Love rather than the love of thought.

M

To Ensoul The World

Holy cow, my mother, sister, counterpart, to reread this is such an experience! Mary Love was finally back today, and I could say so little except for the feeling of support and birth of my soul. To "ensoul" the world! Oh, my living God!

Donny has left and I am alone. I read from my book, *Creation of the New*, for I felt it calling me. I don't know why. I feel that I am unable to grasp or retain *anything*. It "comes in" and I wonder, where did it go? Jesus wonders why I do not trust him to support me in my speaking, and it is hard to when I feel so mute before all of this ... or maybe better said ... behind it. It is as if it goes before me and I will never catch up. As if this is the way it is. "I go before you always, even unto the end of time." It is only with the end of time that we are not going forward in this way of muteness, isn't it? In this way of trying to catch up to what we know? Or is it just that I do?

(Now it appears Donny was not "gone" at all, and I pause a bit to attend to this "here" in which I still abide.)

M

The Childhood of The New

You are thinking of the book you are reading on the Trinity, and Jesus described it well. Your Richard Rohr describes it well.[24] But you are wondering of my place in it, much as you wonder of your place in the world. I had a place. Do not worry about me. Like you, I did not seek recognition but only the opposite, and did not realize my divinity to much greater of an extent than do you. But I recognized my God and our Son, as do you.

My sister, we are all divine. We resist the notion of our divinity because of its association with power, not the opposite. And when there is an inkling of power, that a power flows through you, there is a response that is not one of elation or even thankfulness. It is not fear of the power, not fear of the world's response to it, but a heavy weariness with the world's fascination with, and misunderstanding of, true power.

But you, like me, have this little role to play that is not so little, in recognizing that God's love for us is the presence in which the world exists. The Trinity represents the sacred "one" which you each are, and this oneness manifested. Oneness manifested follows the same pattern as the manifested God.

What is present "here" is an opening in time of which you are a part, as is each one who has released themselves to what is beyond time and space as they know it. This "knowing," in a world

---

24 *The Divine Dance*, SPCL 2016, Richard Rohr with Mike Morrell

of time and space, is not an easy knowing to hold or to carry. It makes your life both blessed and very nearly sacrificial.

M

In every time on Earth there has been a grueling struggle because of time's manifestation, which has steadily and slowly been coming to awareness within the "confines" of form. Yes, time itself is becoming aware. This is what has not been seen. Time is becoming aware of herself. This is not "clock" time, but the "time" of the awareness of a living universe that, like your own body, has formed life without becoming aware of living. A living universe is a responsive universe. Now this is being seen and, in being seen, is coming to life-consciousness.

This is the way of creation!

Remember that feeling and thought, feminine and masculine, birthed the Love of God into form. Jesus passed this actuality of divinity "in form" into the hearts and minds of humanity, and others quickly followed.

But time itself, which you might call the "container" in which the thought of God created, knew not itself . . . as you have not known yourselves. Now is the time in which the universe is becoming conscious of herself as what you call "time," and this conscious awareness of herself, newly birthed, is not so unlike your own.

How do you respond to Mary Love's awareness of who you are, and your awareness of who she is? You grow in that awareness. You grow more fully into yourself when you know and are known, and when you know that you are known. You grow in joy.

Time can now be on your side. The cells of your body (as part of the newly birthing conscious universe) can now "be on your side." It is an apt enough description. Just as you have been conscious without knowing the full extent of your consciousness, so has what we are calling time and "the conscious universe" been slowly awakening to its true nature. You are helping or hindering this advent of consciousness, just as there are those in the world who help and hinder you.

Because you are all newly birthing into consciousness, it is the childhood of The New.

M

The Birthing Consciousness of Time

Holy Mother, I write as I begin my day "beyond sunrise." It was a beauty this morning, understated and still in the midst of rising at 7:30. I am going out today. It will be the first time in a while. The Social Security Office beckons me with the excitement of getting a regular check. And so, I am about to go take a shower. I had a website meeting after our talk yesterday, a meeting in which time did not stretch enough to get a lot done, but in which Steve and I became more comfortable with one another, and after which I felt ill. I went to bed at 7:00 and slept until 6:00. I suspect it was too much for one day. That was a powerful receiving yesterday morning.

Yes, it was exciting, was it not? And difficult to move on from? Difficult to focus narrowly again, and to see time as a constraint? Difficult to remember that time can be on your side? I want you to do your best to remember this now—not as a task but as your way of being freed from the cyclical duties that leave you not the time you desire for creating. When you begin to appreciate time's capacity to expand, you will "find" the time for the expression of what you are coming to know and have come to know. Your early morning thoughts were full, full from the "well of spirit" which can now be likened as well to the birthing consciousness of time. This is the consciousness that will take the world out of time as it has been known.

You are witnessing ideas that were shared with you in A Course of Love *twenty years ago, being passed on, in this time, by "prominent" and innovative thinkers. This is a good thing and a demonstration of the way "your own consciousness" is not yours alone. As you expanded your consciousness, your "idea"— what you "held within your spaciousness consciousness" and only hoped to express anew—began to be expressed. Some of the ideas you discovered for yourself were discovered by others prior to your discovery. You will open doors for each other more and more. This is exciting. And this can prepare you for the way that time will now be on your side. As we bring forth these thoughts and feelings, they arise into time as new truths, and are manifested.*

Do not expect time to treat you as it has in the past when it was not a friend to you. Last night, time was your friend, calling you to rest. Today, let time befriend you through your actions of all kinds. Cease to discriminate or see a difference between "our holy time together" and every moment. Begin to invite the consciousness of "time outside of time" ... which has always been ... into time. Let it help and heal and begin to be aware of itself "here" where its capacity to aid, rectify, and create anew is needed.

Remember that time is on your side and that you are helping it get to know what it can be in this period of its arising in the world of form as what it is. It is "your" consciousness of it—as a living companion—which will flavor it with compassion and, at the same time, appreciation for the urgency of the world's needs. Help birth time outside of time into time with love and care. Mother it into what it will be aware that it is.

M

Self-Love and Suffering

Dearest Holy Mary and Jesus,

I cannot believe it has been five days! My brother sent me here to speak to you of the suffering, my Mary, the suffering of healing. And I feel I must include "the sending" here. It is so beautiful:

M

JOURNAL ENTRY

6:56 and the sky is already lighter than I had hoped it would be when I got here. I set the alarm for 5:45 but stayed in bed until 6:35. It seems like such a short time ago it stayed dark until well after seven.

I had to wipe fog off the window in order to see anything, and I only made one sandwich in not wanting to miss any last bit of my morning's coming of light "out of darkness," which is the theme of this time.

Wouldn't that be it, my brother? This review of every trauma?

There's a crescent moon moving so far toward the west that I can't see it now without craning, and that bright, bright star I've been seeing for a while must be, can only be, *the North Star*—the North Star of *Creation of the New*.

Now my glasses are back off. They are so dirty I can hardly see out of them. I am a mess. Maybe we all have these dark, dirty depths and you just can't see it so well—the light, unless you are coming out of it—the dark.

But with all your help, I still feel like I am getting a little lost! I am not supporting myself enough or letting my soul support me enough. But this is it, right here. Only making one peanut butter sandwich in my rush to come as fast as I can, because I must feel you and my soul, and this is my time, and this is my "winter" place.[25] And so, I am here, my Lord and Brother, in my maudlin state, to ask you what I am not seeing and what I am to do, even though I know you won't tell me. But dear Jesus, will you please be with me? And not let me use you—ever.

The first squirrel is up and about at 7:12.[26] I saw him leaping and grabbed my glasses, thinking he was a big bird! His appearance makes me feel better.

You could never "use" me, my sister. You are a deeply feeling being, and this, whether you realize it or not, is the place you need to be, the seat of your passion and compassion. You want to leave your places of deep feeling—quickly. Feel them all in a rush. But then, as soon as you share a little, you feel vulnerable, and when you feel vulnerable you want to retreat. And then you go to your mind and begin to worry ... and your worry uses you for no end.

Do not worry. Do not worry, my sister! The feelings you are feeling are love of self as you have memo-

---

25 I am speaking, due to the weather, of being inside looking out at the cabin.

26 I did not include the time for this reason, but both the time and the view generally reveal the space in which a response is awaited.

ries arise and look back on all you endured ... alone. I was your comfort then. I am your comfort now. Me in you, and me as me, and me as hundreds of sisters and brothers who feel grateful and "close" to you through our work. Yes. Close to "you." They may not know it, but they do, they are, close to you. They fell within your sphere when they fell within mine through our Course. Each one is now a kindred spirit whether they seem so or not, because, although they may not know this either, they are not neutral about you. They are grateful or envious or full of wonder, or doubt, or questions, or admiration. They are not neutral. Some like to think they are, but they are not. There is, at times, a great desire to remain neutral, to not regard you personally, to still their curiosity, to hear it is not about you but about themselves, or not about you or them but about a universality that keeps love distant.

Remember when, in one long-ago conversation of ours, you cried about your single mother days, as well as the difficulties then present in your life, and I told you to paint a new picture.[27] To feel the support of love is to paint the new picture that is not sanitized. This is the sweetness of love. It does not sanitize. It is not a resume. It is not a list of accomplishments brushed clean of trial and error, of pain and loss. This sanitization of love is what keeps it less than the power that it is.

To endure the pain of love, the dark of love, to come

---

27 See The Jesus Chronicles at mariperron.com

into the light of love, is to cast aside the loneliness of love. You do this by continually revisiting the Oneness where love's loneliness still resides and comes to rest. "Resting in Oneness," is a return to where your journey began, to the original womb of life.

You know this as you comfort yourself by rocking to the heartbeat that we share. "Here," you are embraced in the mutuality of our love and yes, our suffering.

People, each person, has suffered so much that they cannot disregard it, no matter how they try ... until they stop trying. The end of suffering is the beginning of its regard, and the realization of the love always there within it. The love that prays for the end of one's own suffering, prays for the end of suffering of all "in oneself." We are all one Self. We share one story, a story of life, of living. And in this acceptance of life as it is, we embrace suffering, and suffering falls away from us as singular suffering ... as you think of all single mothers, all women raped, all those discriminated against, all those overlooked and unseen, all those who struggle with lack, all those who have hurt and been hurt by those they love, all those who have lied to shield their pain, their embarrassment, their shame, and their hope of being different than they are, different than the circumstances of their lives, so that they can remain true to love, the love they are.

Suffering is a form of self-love when it is recognized as a form of self-love ... as a hope for ease, for honesty, for knowing and being known ... as one truly is!

No one can see suffering truly until they embrace love of self, which is why I began the Course in the way you have always regretted. It is a paradox my sister, of not being able to love oneself, and so suffering lack of love, which is impossible. And in coming to know love, suffering love's embrace and the potential to heal into love, which is a form of suffering. Go now to our mother.

M

Mary, it feels such a far cry from our last visit.

Yet it is not. It is not at all. The conscious universe, newly birthing into awareness of its consciousness, needs all the love you can give to it to counterbalance the hate. To know itself, as it is known by love, is what awareness is, not what consciousness without awareness is. Your own consciousness is not yet continuously aware, and yet you do not want to strive for this. Let it come. The consciousness of time is not going to strive for knowing it is love and capable of love's knowing. It is going to be infiltrated by your awareness of its birthing along with you.

You have not remained aware these last five days, except for moments. You are feeling vulnerable, and whether you realize it or not, vulnerability is part of the growth of awareness, and not to be feared, covered over, or hidden from. We bring each other to awareness. Your awareness of your squirrels and birds blesses them, and this you have come to feel, as their awareness of you blesses you.

Being aware that you do not know is also an awareness, the beginning of awareness. You said this just yesterday, "I don't know." Good for you! You do not have to know! As "time" does not have to know, as the new babe does not have to know. Love brings awareness to life. This is what we do. We bring awareness into being as a loving companion to life ... which you also are, dear one. Which you also are.

And so, you have come to me to hear of suffering healing. All healing comes as suffering. Can this cycle end?

The beginning of the end is in our vision—our vision of the beginning of the end of time "as it has been known." You see, "knowing" has always been key and remains key. But coming to know is slow going on Earth, even with divine help. This help, always provided, is coming into its time of fullness because of the awareness that time is being offered. You will help to expand this awareness.

I have closed the blinds against the sun's glare and view now only the lovely shadows of my dear trees, seen through windows fogged with cold and drizzling light. It soothes me, my Mother, to see this one square of time, this one familiar plot of ground, today white with snow and cold. I miss my Mary Love and am afraid to miss her in a time when she is needed by so many.

This is the perfect time to call out "to" time in love and ask for time's assistance. Ask and ask, in love, for time's assistance. Welcome time to work with you and not against you. Appreciate the "time" you have here and the exquisite potential of this time. See time's beauty as you see the design of sun on snow. "All" is enveloped in time. Time's awareness is beginning to peek through, into time ... through you. Through your awareness of time's potential consciousness of itself in Love, time becomes aware. Show it its beauty as you see it in your day, through your eyes, your musings. Befriend time and let time befriend you.

Time outside of time holds the universe in its loving embrace, all the heavens cooperating, intermingling, in relationship. Only on your humanized strip of time does time enter the concreteness of form and meet resistance. Do you see? "You" make yourself concrete. "You" make yourselves formidable "objects."

Until you become spacious.

In spaciousness there is no resistance, no concreteness. There is no measuring of time, plotting with and against time, shaking one's fist at time, railing at the container of time in which you are born, live, suffer, and die—only sometimes adding Love: born love, living love, suffering love, dying into new love.

And so, you may ask, where in this spaciousness lies the need of other things we have spoken of, such as "anchors" of The New?

M

Anchoring the Passage Into a New Age

As the "son of God" came to anchor the truth of who you are into consciousness, (one in being with God), so the "daughters of God" now are called upon to anchor the fulfillment of the time of Jesus with the passing into The New, the new age that we are calling "the way of Mary." This is a move from the masculine to the feminine of time, an anchoring of the infinite awareness of the consciousness of creation . . . in time. We are knitting together time, with time outside of time; birthing time's awareness of itself as helpmate to human expansion—through spaciousness, into spaciousness.

There is, here, a tremendous connection to both healing and suffering. Again, one would not exist without the other. They are knitted together, birthed together "in time." All concrete crumbles eventually. The concreteness of human form, bounded within skin, born into time, and dying out of time, cannot fail to change as time itself changes. "Thought forms" are the barriers that are like unto concrete dams. They give form its solidity.

Do you see? Born into time. Dying out of time. Life existing "in" time.

But life began as, and can return to being, creation of The New! Earth time began as an evolving, living consciousness, held "by" the awareness of time outside of time, on the home of plan-

et Earth. And on Earth this drama of evolution has played out within "time outside of time's" embrace of it. This is the embrace of Love, the very time from which you hear these words and are held in relationship with me ... also known as the Earth Mother, the embodiment and the over-body of the feminine principle of fertility.

And now, you who live on The Earth call yourself not only human but "mortal," which is associated with murder and death, as if you come here to die rather than to live. Nothing could be farther from the principle of fertility or the feminine face of God. Fertility is synonymous with plentitude, fruitfulness, a richness of life.

M

Earth Time Holds Love Incarnate

And so, it is only appropriate that the feminine face of love now embrace "Earth time" and love it into conscious awareness of what it holds: love incarnate.

Time—driven from the beginning, by the masculine: in mind and might and strength, driven to be conqueror of nature in support of mans' small life and offspring—birthed necessity and struggle into the Eden of the world. Humankind continued in this way, the way of the conqueror of time and nature, a battle it is losing.

Consider this truth or another rendition of myth. It matters not. But consider it. This losing battle. All battles are losing battles.

People are longing for time for love.

Suffering is a longing for time to love. Healing is a giving over of time to love. Such is the time in which you and I sit together on Earth in time outside of time. Here, love reigns in spacious consciousness, devoid of objects, populated only by the light and energy of faces of love that show the way. Still no "two" the same, my children. Still within a multiplicity of relationship far beyond what you can imagine, my Holy Ones. Still, even with the impartiality of time which "has been," making each "loss" of time a gain in love outside of time ... until finally, the age is here in which the impartiality of time will gain consciousness and seek only love. Love is the homing beacon calling all to itself.

M

Love's Warmth and the Embrace

You are hungry for love, to be known as you are known by love. To feel love's warmth rather than the chill of indifference, or worse, conflict. You can never hear enough that you are loved, but the words of love repeated are not this hearing.

There is a coldness in the world in this time that hungers, as you hunger individually and collectively for the warmth and fecundity of love, for the deliciousness of it . . . like the scent of warm berries. You are hungry for love and yet have a hard time hearing of it, have a hard time admitting to your need of it, have a hard time hearing others being praised with words of love. You hunger for love's admiring. Words of love cannot be spoken in enough ways to fill you. Love and thankfulness, appreciation for who you are, these are what are needed and are needed by all, if "thingness" is to be transcended.

What you hold to yourself you imbue with spirit. What is holding "you" imbues you with spirit. This is the embrace. It is mutual—each to each—as "eachness replaces thingness."[28] *What is directed by each to one another is of love to love. This is so, even when you know it not, because you are love.*

The need is still here, the need to hear words of love spoken. You are love, you are light, you are the rays of love blessing the

---

28 See ACOL C:20.39

world, the love that holds hands, the love that wipes tears, the love that hides under the covers of darkness.

M

ISE

Arise and face the day of love's being. Rise from your beds to face love. Hide no more beneath sleep's blankets. Rise to Love. Rise and be the risen Love. Rise and be who you are. Who you are is love. You sleep in love. You wake in love. Because you are love. Because you are loved. Because you are loveable and as innocent as a babe in arms. You are that babe as was my son. Born in utter innocence and free of any stain or capability of sin. Your misperceptions are forgiven as quickly as they occur, and brought now, to the light of Love in time where you can see that this is so, where you can see that you are that which you are and have always been.

Grieve your dark days only to awaken from them with greater depths of compassion, with greater awareness of love's many expressions, and let them rise from you, and with you, into time free of the concreteness of the past. Offer these qualities of your Self to time itself so that it may hold open human time's awareness. You are not separate from anything, even the illusion of time that "you" have made.

So, bring it with you. Bring all with you in the fullness of time. Invite all to rise with you in love for love's sake. For love's sake, rise to end the suffering of the human condition. Rise to end racism, injustice, abuse, torture, and war. Rise to end the lack that does not need to be. Rise along with time to call on time's ability to heal all wounds, to provide for all. Rise to meet the consciousness *of Mother Earth and the love of "this time" and "this place." Seek no more for what will be. Love into existence what Is.*

Speak your own words of love. Raise your voice to love. Love All.

You began hearing of this in my son's words: the fullness of time.

"In this time of unity, dedicate all thought to unity. Accept no separation. Accept all choices. Thus are all chosen in the fullness of time."[29]

It is time to usher in the "fullness of time."
The Covenant of the New is the awareness that this is the time to end all time . . . as it has been. Not to end "life" but to end the interval in which "time" lost awareness of itself, as have you. The time in which what God the Father made, and God the Mother blessed with conception, returns to its true nature in the here and now in which you exist. This is what is meant by a time of no time.

"This is the agreement God asks of you, your part of the shared agreement that will fulfill the promises of your inheritance. This is the Covenant of the New in which you honor your agreement to bring heaven to earth and to *usher in* the reign of Christ. To *usher in* is to show the way, to cast your palms upon the path of your brothers and sisters. Do you not see that your acceptance of this promise is the acceptance of your own promise? Do you not see that acceptance of the new and denial of the old is the necessary

---

29 See ACOL T4:6.8

forerunner of our work together in establishing the Covenant of the New?"[30]

Let go the pattern of thought, and a new pattern will emerge out of the heart of love. Trust that this will be so. Trust that all thought can be transformed by love and that new patterns, divine patterns, will arise. Trust, and anchor this trust in the world so that the new time can come to be, in Love.

M

---

[30] ACOL D:2.23

An Opening in Time

FEBRUARY 2019

My Mother, speaking of time ...

I wish to end my own "busyness." This seems a small thing to bring to you, but it is a big thing to me right now. I have been working to close out the old as a prelude to welcoming The New, and it seems never ending, this work. Each day I think I will be done with it and it continues. It makes me concerned that I will not be able to go on.

I was "working" with someone the other day who wanted to open and close our session with prayer. Another person wrote to me wondering about *A Course of Love's* way of prayer. When the person I worked with prayed before we began, I did not object, and the words were fine, but it bothered me a little for reasons I can't name. It felt like it was a thing done. A thing to do. Not arising naturally, in other words. I thought of everything being a prayer, my life being a prayer, the constancy of our acts of giving and receiving as one, our every thought a prayer. I could chastise myself and say my every thought is not a prayer, but that would be, I feel, the old way. I pray still, at night before bed, and at other times ... when I feel so moved. I feel the sense of prayer in the glory of my mornings, when I write, when my friends and I share our hearts (or I feel it right afterwards). I am talking to time and asking for spaciousness, but I am having difficulty with the old and new sitting here, together with me, even the loving old. Ideas of prayer are only a small part of it. Maybe that's all it is. Old and New.

And yet, you see it, don't you? The old. The New. This is what must be seen before it can be left behind. This is why you are seeing it.

I want to just leave the old behind without the "clean up." That is what it feels like. Like I'm cleaning up a mess of things, and it is so wearying.

Yes, the "mess of things" is wearying. And you are seeing it. Your Mary Love is seeing it. The world is seeing it. This preponderance of "things" that shield you from spaciousness.

You have at times dismissed those who walk away, and yet sometimes this is the only way that they can escape the "mess of things" long enough to come into spaciousness fully. Your years of "morning time" have been your opening to spaciousness. Even amidst the things of time, you received A Course of Love—received Jesus in your heart—in his voice and your own. "Here" you have your time with me. To do this "within time" is sometimes a great weight, a pressure on you. We know this and want to assure you of the incredible nature of this exertion that is actually extension. This is one of the most significant of openings for time's awareness of its own consciousness and ability to participate in creation of The New.

$\mathcal{M}$

Imagine human-time like a closed circle and what you do causing an opening in that circle that is like a vortex. We are speaking of an opening in time itself and a movement, a swirling movement, coming into what has become as still and barren as the air in a room closed-up for centuries. The great discoveries in caves are like this action. The air swirls in on what had been entombed. Some forms, when meeting this new air, crumble. Others, once rid of dust, shine forth again.

At the points of this collision of The New and old, you feel this swirl. You feel neither here nor there. And then to turn to those things that are the concrete of the old, is like being hit by debris swirling within a tornado. You are and have been heroic and mighty in your faithfulness. We love you so much and I am saying to you now that your endeavors in The New will not be the same. You will not be tossed by the storms of transition much longer, begotten one, nor will those who, knowingly or not, are companioning you into The New.

Continue to befriend your human time and also, my sweet one, begin to see that you do not need to attend to the former things as much as you imagine. The matters of living ... yes. The matters of what is the dying way ... no.

Thank you, Mother, for these words that make me feel such gratitude, and that let me know you recognize "me," in this way that I have felt, but have not had acknowledged. Thank you so very much.

My daughter, the last thing I want to say to you is that our gratitude to you may have to be enough. There is gratitude, yes, as you have been given, for the sharing of our words, but few of those who receive them have had the experience that you have had with them, and know not of psychic heroism, which in the past was called mysticism or saintliness or lunacy and was also unrecognized so very often, until after the death of the one given over to this service to humanity.

The time is different now because so many are experiencing that which is opening this monistic influx, revealing the unity of all that exists ... even in human time. You will feel this growth more and more, and join, more and more, with the creators of it. This will soothe your tortured body and mind and bring solace, and joy, to your heart. You will find you have a great capacity for joy and that you greatly enjoy the leaving behind of the old and its "busyness."

You are heading into the great departure.

The Great Departure

You are healing into the great departure and the perfect life situation has arisen with which we can work with you. It is time to embrace your power, to heal into your power. The amplified waves that you heard and felt last night were an influx of your power. You see your power as being in your words, our words, but it is an expansive power and it comes from love. And so, in this troublesome situation that has arisen, there is a need for the very combining that will usher in The New. An identification of "the old," and a denial of its power is the first step. The second step is finding a way to do this identification and this naming of "the old," with love. The third step is identifying The New and proclaiming it with both love and power. But you must start with love, even if it is love that arises out of anger. Lead with Love always.

This you did last night at my urging.

Now you have identified "the old"—with love. What is the old you have identified? A "power over" old. This is a great power that has gained credence even in what are called spiritual circles by virtue of . . . let us say . . . convenience. When one does not want to consider more than a single option, it is a matter of inconvenience. Options might require a change of mind or actions. The call to new thought and action (or no thought and action!) are a great piece of the puzzle.

The "action" needed to address the power over is also an inconvenience.

Yes! It is the last thing I want to do!

You will also want to consider the spiritually correct attitude that translates into a virtue of the well-intentioned and the peace loving, and a vice in the one bound to truth, accuracy, honor, and reverence for a "higher truth." This may be a matter of practicality or of arrogance, (on either side), or of a desire for peace that sees not the consequences of a "giving up or over" to the easiest way. It can also be a desire for self-assertion. "I'm the one in charge here." At times it is of both ends of the spectrum.

The insidiousness of the problem is that it is not seen. This is the very insidiousness of "the old" that causes it to remain. "Deny the old." How do you do this? Do you turn the other way, or do you confront the old? Do you "confront" the old or do you let "the old" be revealed? What is being revealed in this situation that you currently face? It is an invaluable revealing. It may just be the key to your departure.

In these ventures that go about as if they are "the norm," there is an inherent allegiance to "the old." It is not the "action" so much as the "intention," or the way that the action is gone about that causes the harm. This is the "power over" that you have recognized. It is often not only a matter of following a way of old but a matter of revenge or protection, which always have to do with woundedness.

You have seen this in yourself and part of your reason for being here is to let all go but love. You are here, not only for your love of God and humanity, but for your love of words and their power to transform, your love of writing and its creative expansion of *ideas, your love of books and their friendliness ... their ability to befriend you. There is a trust you place in your books, in their authors, in the way they convey what they do.*

There is a bond between the reader and the Word, especially these Holy Words. There is a bond between all creative partners. It is a needed bond. It acknowledges the weaving together of the art and its manifestation.

M

Power and the Time to Act

Dear Holy Mary,

It must be a week or more. A long time. I have just had a dialogue with Kate in Australia. There was a sense of The New that was so strong, like we were twin vortexes of newness. Pops are now going on outside, as if of fireworks. As I look out, searching for the source of the noise, I see an image of this swirling energy. There is something going on. It continues ... the popping sound. What could be causing it?

You were so right when you said I was in the perfect life situation to heal into my power. It took me until today to see it. I suddenly knew (the popping continues) that I do have power. I have written of the power-over situation as if I am the one crushed beneath its weight, but I also have power. It came only hours ago. I know it is true. Nothing is different and everything is different. I have power. And you ask that it be a power that leads with love. Oh, my God, it is so much easier to imagine leading with love when you are the power, than when you are not. It is all the difference in the world. It is mind-boggling, like a switch thrown somewhere, and suddenly I see. No. It is not as I thought it was. I *can* hold the power. (More and more popping.)

And hence I wonder, "Now what?" I have never been here before! I have never felt my power like I do tonight.

Now is the time to act. Act from power with love. This is what all of this came to show you. It is an amazing turn around, and you will not take long to grow used to it.

You love into newness, my daughter. You love into newness.

But you know how people can sound so arrogant with love!

You will not sound arrogant. Let the dust of the whirlwind settle. You know now how fragile are the hearts that bear the old. You have felt the weight of the old all your life, and keenly, so keenly, so physically, mentally, soulfully, these past weeks. Yet even with all your complaining and worry, you have felt a "sense" of love beneath what the frightened ones reveal to you. You even sense the fear. This "sensing" of fear is exceptionally valuable now. You once, in your own embrace of fear, could not sense the fear in those you faced. Know that where you see arrogance, there is fear.

And so, you have come to know not to have arrogance. This is what you worry that exclaiming over The New you have experienced and moved into will be taken as—arrogance. Where you see arrogance, know that there is fear. Do not give fear cause to grow. Be gentle. Ease fears. This is your real power. It will be mighty.

M

Rest in Love

My Holy Mother, I find it hard to see myself as the easer of fears. I have only rarely been on that side of any situation. With Henry it was at its greatest. Maybe also with Dad. That protection of the young and old.

I do not feel strong enough now. Can you help me?

Begotten one, yes, of course I will help you. Let me hold you here, in this sacred place for a little bit. Let yourself feel held.

(After a few minutes ...)

Did you see that you are much better at embracing than being embraced, even in your imagination? Let your shoulders relax. Return to the image of yourself as a babe lovingly held by your own mother, by Madeline, a woman who let you love her for a long little while.

Now you have seen an image and know that your greatest comfort was in lying on the couch when you were sick, with a blanket and pillow and your mom going about her day. Not tending to you but being there. Making her everyday noises, singing "I love you so much it hurts me." Rattling pans. Moving up and down the stairs, the smell of the iron and of starch. Aromas from the kitchen. You were not separate. You were part of it all, but the attention was not on you. You had a Self and it felt honored in

*this way of being left alone but embraced, as if by the house itself
and its sounds as well as your mother's. It was an autonomous
feeling of love and yet one of being part of everything.*

You are so right. That is the way I feel at rest in love. Not with attention. Not with absence. With a quite simple "being together."

Yes, my Mari. Autonomy and togetherness. No matter that you are part of everything and everything part of you, this sacred aloneness is your comfort, the security from which you realize that you exist in the embrace. You do not want to be smothered with attention, nor left out of the picture of the whole. That is what you felt on the couch on Smith Avenue. You were left alone but were tended to and you took it all in . . . "in." You heard every creak, the rhythm of the furnace, the press and steam of the iron, the release of the vacuum seal of the refrigerator, the scrape of the chair as your mother sat down in the kitchen, the scratch of her pen as she wrote a note, the tick of the clock. And this you have transferred beautifully to Henry whose way is much like your own. You co-exist without . . . "fuss."

And this is what you gravitate back to. The familiar sights and sounds and rhythm of life. These comfort you.

Yes.

Imagine me with you as your mother once was, a part of the household's rhythm, for such I am, with no invasion whatsoever until you welcome it. But I am here. I am like the house that holds you safe from the elements, like its warmth and provision. We rest within the same tent.

We take in all its details and know when something is out of order . . . because of our familiarity, bred of love and a togetherness that extends to the inanimate: the rhythm and scents are that of which we have acute awareness. We are the first to hear the leaks in the roof.

There is always room for this combination of what "is" physically and what we, in relationship to all that is, "take in" from acts of the mundane. You have always loved the sacrament of Holy Communion because, you have said, you could imagine Jesus at the last supper, making a metaphor of what was at hand. This is what we do here "in form" to demonstrate what is both within form and beyond form. Do not forget the "within" when you speak of the beyond. The within is an internal beyond, an acceptance of metaphor and of all that cannot be seen but Is.

M

eing Rocked

MARCH, 2019

Dear One, I have begun to move away from what is old in my life. I can feel it.

Who knew it would be so hard! My eyes tear up with the senselessness of it all but also with a knowing that I can't go another day. "The old" has become like living a lie. I just feel in anguish with my desire for The New. I desire to approach the way of the creator, to come home to the self I am as a creative self. It is as if this is something I cannot do in the world's way of time and so it reminds me, again, to invite time to be my friend "in The New." I so desire to be a creator. To create! I have missed it, my Holy Mother, like a missing of myself. Yes, this is what it is. A missing of myself. Here I am, newly birthing my soul and this new time, and I have found myself missing. Will you help me?

Yes, I am rocking you, my child, as you have been rocked since the onset of A Course of Love. *Rocked from the heart within. Rocked with steadiness, which does not mean with dullness or oldness or lethargy or lack. You are rocked, and you know this, by creative love. Love of creativity. Creation itself.*

Here is the world of ideas and of ideas becoming manifest. While you want to "create out of your own being," you also want to be part of creation of The New. Do they seem incompatible to you? They are not. Your own self is not mute within what is created from our shared voice. Yes, here we share. This your brother has long called you to—this sharing. And the act of sharing, as are so many of your actions, is expanding. Right now, as you rock, you are sharing in an encompassing vibratory field of heart energy. Creative energy. You hear the sound of your heart being in your ears. It is our heart. Listen to it.

It quieted, Holy One. As soon as I began to listen it quieted. Now it is perceptible again, but I notice how it changes as I begin to type. It is very steady in between. But it still is different than when I began. Gentler perhaps.

It is amazing, is it not, how much is heard when you listen. And now you want to listen to yourself and we have started with the beat of your heart. Remember your choice for your Centering Prayer word and its relation to the heart. You become so aware of it in your stillness.

Now you are realizing that each time you close your eyes and still your fingers, the sound is there, and yet, as you are leaving off of my words and coming into your own space, there is a lessening so pronounced that it is as if you cannot find it. Behind your closed eyelids there is movement, as though even your eyes ask, where has gone the heartbeat. And then it returns, yes?

Now "you" want to be heard. You want to hear "your" heartbeat, and desire to have your heart heard.

Yes! Every woman I know is waiting to be heard. It is as though we never realized how silenced we have been.

I know, my Mari. I know.

M

Be still my heart. Do you know that expression?

Yes. It is one of those that has been with me all my life, but I don't know from where. Poetry?

We are going to take this a little differently, as in, Be you still my heart? Now the sound of it is louder again, is it not? We are asking now, consulting with the heart. Are you there? Are you still my heart? We are addressing the heart as we have addressed time. As I have asked you to address your soul. There is the thundering heart and the quiet heart. Invite your heart into quiet restfulness with you. Oneness with you. Who is held in that beating? What pulse are you loyal to? The pulse of the old or the pulse of The New? Where lies your creativity? In the pulse of the old or the pulse of The New?

You look back on your creativity and wish for it again. Look forward, creative one. Look forward. Look forward newly to creation of The New. Do not look over your shoulder and down the way. Look forward.

The inward is now the realm of the forward motion that meets with that of time outside of time and mingles with it. Your heart's beat is within you! Within you! And how seldom do you realize this or the state of all that lies beneath your skin? The workings of the body, now that it is one with you, are miraculous in a new way. Yes, in a new way.

What the inner ear hears affects the brain. (And now no activity is happening. None, not a sound.) Chemicals fire within you from thought as well as words spoken.

But you head for the silence. "You" head for the silence. I want you to heed this small demonstration and to know that we are lighting up new areas within you, from toes to temple. I want you to know that silence is not stillness of body. It is another kind of stillness. I want you to begin to listen for it. To grow more aware of the connection between the ear and the heart. The listening ear, the waiting heart. Now you have greater pounding in your right ear.

I know you have not had great interest in the body, but we are not speaking of the kind of interest that is most associated with it—its care and feeding, its exercise, its agility. We are speaking of its receptivity. Its availability for all that is coming in the way of The New. This will have to do with the new creativity ... at which your heart just ... leapt! This is the way forward. You do not want to go back, you want to go forward.

Watch, listen, feel the tempo of your heart and where it makes itself aware to you. This is not an exercise, but an awareness, an observation, a way to invite the measure of the soul that rests within. The soul that newly sees with your eyes. The eyes that newly see with your soul. This is going to be your creativity alert system, your herald, your invitation to ensoul your (hard chest beat) ... all that you create. (More chest beats.)

I put a hand on my heart and my heart leapt and my ear ... I do not know what to say it did, but it responded.

You will not be able to begin now, as you are "thinking about it." This is not to be thought about. But remember, you will ensoul with what you create, and your heart and your ear (the right particularly) will be your guide. The hand to the heart is also dear. It is welcome. It is the way of the pledge, of faithfulness. Be faithful to the heart of The New and listen. Listen "in." Do not expect it always to be the way of hearing as it has been. Do not expect what *is outside of the body not to infiltrate, or what is within the body not to emanate.*

Creativity is not only as you have imagined it to be. Let your imagination explore creativity newly. We are, after all, creating The New.

ℳ

Be Still and Know

After we had our dialogue early on Saturday, I had my early evening call with Kate, where it was her Sunday morning. During it, I shared with her a quote from Cynthia Bourgeault's book on Centering Prayer. I went to it after our talk earlier in the day, my Mother, because I thought I remembered something in it that related to what you shared with me, possibly about the ear's connection to the heart. I never found it, but found memories flooding in. Suddenly I recalled what got me started in Centering Prayer.

It was when I left my job at the University of Minnesota to "work for God," a year or so before ACOL announced itself. I visited Fr. Adrian looking for suggestions. He got me to teach CCD religion, but also suggested Centering Prayer. Sometimes I forget how clueless I was and that this did not all happen in a straight line! I joined a Centering Prayer group that met in the parish center. I don't know if there were books on this practice by anyone other than Fr. Thomas Keating back then.

Oh Mary, it doesn't seem like it was over twenty years ago—not at all! And in another way, it feels like a different lifetime.

Although I didn't find what I was looking for, I read Kate this quote from Bourgeault's *The Heart of Centering Prayer*. "The Heart," the heart of it, my Mother! She writes: "In its spiritual capacity, the heart is fundamentally a homing beacon, allowing us to stay aligned with those 'emanations from more subtle levels of existence,' ... and hence follow the authentic path of our own unfolding."[31]

Kate and I had been speaking of changes to consciousness within matter when I heard coming from my own mouth: "Maybe we're looking in the wrong place—and it is here in us. How many times do we hear "it is within you?""

If I am trusting of my body now, these feelings I have had of dire threat, great risk, which I feel reached their zenith last night, and that I feel almost depleted from this morning, have been real communication. "The body knows." And since I can't remember what I write here for more than minutes, it is only now that I realize we took a turn to the body yesterday.

My body now gently swirls as I review. It is not the rock. Not forward and back. It is to the right and it moves in a circle—like the cyclone or the vortex.

Can you prepare me, Holy One, for the challenges ahead?

Begotten one, you are done with preparing now. You know a place of deep absorption and a place where your mind is flashing around. You are in "flashing" time now. It is not that unlike the days when you would run from the grocery store for being overwhelmed by too many choices. Too much is literally on your mind. When there are many choices, no one can see their way out. It is one of the most anxiety producing features of this time, and you have long recognized it. "Many choices, all the same." Choices, in other words, that make no difference. What you know you need now is a choice, and a way of conveying that choice, that will make a difference.

---

[31] Bourgeault, C. *The Heart of Centering Prayer*, Shambala Boulder, 2016, p.61, referencing Kabir Helminski, a modern Sufi master.

Choices that make no difference. Boy, I am familiar with those!

Be still and know, my Mari. Be still and know. Agitation is perplexing, not clarifying. It ties you down rather than frees you. And you want to be free. You are sure you must be free for what is next. You are considering ending the fight and moving on. And then you wonder about those who have bravely stood up and said, "No more."

What hearing you say, "No more," brings up, is not thought of a new boldness, but the powerless feeling of saying "No," and having it ignored.

How can I be so thankful and so irritated and so clear and so baffled? I can't stop, my Mother. I'm going over it all again and again and again, hoping I will see something I have not yet seen. How did I get here? I feel disempowered and vulnerable, separated from my calling and a relationship I can't be separated from.

A "vision" is not a plan. This much I can see. Yet "plans" are hatched and proceed, and I try to accept that everyone has their part. It's just that, in this stillness, the question comes forward: What becomes of my part? The part I shared with Jesus? What will become of the part I share with you? And what gets lost?

Isn't it our union?

My heart is so tender that tears fall from my eyes . . . thankful tears . . . because you ask about "me" in a way that assures me that my way is not inconsequential. You ask me to speak up for our hearts and our union. You ask me to draw our companions to The New. I know I have to find a new way to do so.

But you have already stopped carrying on in that old way. Do you not see this?

I guess I don't see how to carry on in a new way.

You do not know that this is what we are doing, my Mari? This is what we are doing. This is your home. This is where you have already gathered your people, this is where your people will find you ... and themselves. And then they will know.

M

The Sacred Heart

Dearest Mary and Jesus,

To feel my own sacred heart. To feel it in communion with another's sacred heart ... even through space and time. Oneness to Oneness.

You know I feel a "coming on" before hearing from you, and how much I enjoy the feeling and how (and this is brand new in the moment) being with you is like that memory of my mother. How near and attentive you are, and part of the house (and the cabin's) rhythm.

And only now am I remembering that you spoke of it, Holy Mary! It came from you, and I forgot, and then remembered. And then before that, it came out of my own being, and then it became my own realization.

I liken it to the imaginal realm somehow, this feeling of presence that is "here," in the privacy of my own sacred heart and your own. My alone time in the cabin that is accompanied. The feel of welcome, hospitality, and sacred privacy combined. It is what I love, and it is glorious.

I am coming home to what I love.

Yes, my daughter.

From here, we turn our gaze to the heart once again, the new heart—the shared heart. The shared heart that comes in times of sacred privacy and rests in union, as you rest in union with your cabin, your quiet home, and memories of your childhood home.

Even now you can rest in those remembrances of childhood where they exist in you.

Here is where you are apart from the unwelcome, even of your thoughts. Here is where you welcome what belongs.

You are apart from company, from the unauthorized, and every once in a while, apart from your own unauthorized thoughts. The Author is the One in a way that is like the cabin, your home, your memory of home. There is a "holding within" that is of the One. You are held. You are safe.

The holding of the One encompasses everything and is the constant in the variable. As your brother shared, "The constant does not become variable because variability exists."[32] You are beginning now to live within the constant of wholeness even as the variability of human experience swirls around you.

"Moments" of experiencing that which is constant are of the beyond within you. Moments extended into minutes are near to miraculous in your experience of them. They are not inconsequential for being short. They are monumental because, in your awareness of them, they are recognized, and allow what we are sharing. This is what those who discount you do not know. The One Voice readied you and "then" spoke to you. Each sharing reflected what you were ready to hear. Look back and see how your readiness grew and be gladdened, begotten one.

Readiness is the beginning that, if one is devoted, will extend into awareness. I choose my words to address the heart that beats and is felt in the act of devotion, the consecration of the individual heart to the One heart. The sustenance given there. The Agnus Dei. The gentle liberation. The spark of a true and liberated

---

32 See ACOL D:Day27.12

*one in the world creates an opening for all. Minutes no less than
months contain this awareness. An opening has been made.*

M

Mirroring an Ensouled World

Your heart holds a reflection of your soul. The cells in your body, and their interaction, mirror the activity in the heavens. You are not separate from anything.

As you free your attention you become aware "inside" of what is outside and can feel the beyond which you are held within. An ensouled world is one that can be mirrored to you and by you— one to another.

The true individual is undivided. The true individual is inseparable from the whole. The whole is, in this way, reflected in the particular and the individual where it can be seen one to another. One-to-one is the way. Each one complete in her creation; his creative living of his own idea; her idea the one out of which she births.

The vision of the imaginal realm is reflected vision. It is a crystalline reflection. This vision holds the particular and the universal. The particular, rather than the universal or the general, is the leading edge, the key to awareness of the whole. This has been mercilessly forgotten and dismissed in this age of the spiritual collective, and has allowed the absolute of the particular, this distinction within the whole, to devolve into the absolute ego. Such sustained particularity is now accredited only to those who rise to the level of power or fame—and so those who aspire to no fame and who fear their own power, dismiss their particularity, just as do those who aspire to no ego. The dismissal of particularity is a sad forgetting of one's Self and the power of us who can only know and "be known" in the particular.

There is no "universal" voice that can speak to you. No universal voice that can be heard. No universal voice exists. To hear is a particular act. To listen is a particular act. To see is a particular act. To speak is a particular act.

To speak is a particular act. I am speaking to you. You are listening to me. There is no nature of being that does not have particularity, as evidenced by your DNA. And so, you begin to see the power of the demonstration of one-to-one. This is the mirroring, the reflection of the way of Mary. The "blending" that you have at times felt is of the joining of one-to-one that is like you looking in your actual mirror to greet your soul. It is two in union. But particularity is not lost.

The duad is irreducible. It is not duality. It is union. Two "together." Without "more than one" there is no uniting to be done, no unity. Unity is joining in togetherness. It is acknowledging one's own being and having one's own being acknowledged. It is acknowledging another's being and having the other being know of the acknowledgment.

The image of God, which is awaited in time outside of time, is that of human in divine and divine in human. It is an intermingling and acknowledgment of two. Here we find our completion and our companion. The duad that is irreducible. Wholeness.

A wholeness that is ever changing.

M

xperience

Dearest Ones,

I am beginning to see that I have been taken to this place of realization, even though I have no words for what I have realized.

To realize is to make real and this is what is happening. Words are not the truth of what is happening but the expression of it. As you have seen, they often lag behind the encounter, at times by greater lengths than others. This is not a failure of words but the onset of experience of what the words might one day convey. Do not push for words before their time. Let experience guide you.

Experience is often associated with "attempts to do" and so also with fear. This is not the experience of which we speak. The experience we speak of is not of trying, or "trying something out," so as to see if it "works." We speak of experience as you know your daily experience of the sun's rising. We speak of experience as participation in, engagement with, a communing.

Experience is the realm in which no two minutes are the same. It is constant newness, which is why you try not to look at the keys as you watch the sun rise. To look down for a moment is to miss, or "step out" of the experience.

Many step out for the entirety of life. This minimizes significance itself.

Mary, my husband has a deposition this morning. He told me he is nervous and hates being nervous. I do not think I ever heard him say that he is nervous. Not once in the nearly 40 years I have known him. It felt so good to have him say this to me. He let me "in" to something he was feeling. And I have no idea why I'm speaking of this at this moment.

You all look forward to moments of such closeness, moments that are, at times, revealed in simple declaratory statements like this one. Some such moments may change your life. And so particular ones, as this one of which you are aware in your life today, stand out, and there comes to be an alertness to them.

This is not the natural "coming on" that you feel when you are aware of inner change in the making, or of an idea, or of the imaginal realm. This is your natural "life on the ground" awareness—the intimate revelations that have the ability to influence your life and relationships. The natural is always true in a familiar and cherished way that you can recognize.

What would happen if more "life on the ground" times were taken into the natural realm? If more events were seen in the same way as the heightened sense of awareness that births an idea? The nature of life on the ground reflects your nature. You are in a movement, now, to the freedom in which life on the ground situations will be unrestricted by your ideas of what they will be. What if you were able to see all of your "life on the ground" encounters in the natural realm?

M

All the ways of The New are movements. They cannot be concretized and be of The New. They happen. This is the reason that your brother and I speak of movement, being, and expression. It is the way of The New.

Movement is the great departure. It is to "depart" from where you stand in history, in the program, in the plan, in a certain stage of structured time, what I have called the concreteness of form in time: the structure, the edifice of time.

Particularly now, as time outside of time is swirling into you and into the time that has been—a point in time structured "by" your very thought forms, it is essential for you to grasp, if you will, the "time" in which "movement" brings "being" into its time of "expression." Here we take movement away from the organized efforts of change, or the drive to get from here to there, and see movement more as the rhythm and character of what is happening, as within a symphony that quavers and spins, trills and dips. Hear the cadence of the themes and composition, the dynamic nature of that which is set in motion. Listen to the pulsating energy that time now is.

There have always been peoples who saw and heard this vibrant nature of life outside of the order that darkened time. These were people who stood beyond that which insisted that all fall into shadow but man's will; that all that showed the way to power, even spiritual power, be dominated by this same will, and entombed along with man—shielded from both light and life.

M

Creation of a New Language

We let language serve us now as we speak again of these ancient knowings, come and gone, but not lost. You listen to the arising of the new language as it summons you, as you are a creator and a poet of language. For each to see themselves thus is our aim, for the creation of a new language can infuse life itself with the poetry of Sophia; the poetry of creation Herself. This is a poetry of desire for life rather than for death. A poetry of awe and reverence rather than disdain.

Those who choose death know not what they choose. Those who choose life know only longing for life and the living compassionate truth that is there in its sharing.

The alchemy needed in the language of this new time is that of replacing facts. Facts were the hardened way of the old. The New is as fluid as is poetry. The New is unrefined. It is magnificence and depth that cannot be grasped but can be held gently, ever so gently, ever so lightly, as it comes into being without hardening.

The New is the rising of the Bread of Life.

M

The Irreducibility of the Two Is the One

March 26th and a cabin sunrise in near dark, the sky streaked with lines of pink and coral and fuchsia and mellow yellow.

"We have to do this again," I think I just heard from you, Holy Mary.

Yes, we are repeating. We are doing this again. And no one else can do what you can do. The means may not be the same, the category will never be, nor the essence of the two joined as one as we are. The uniqueness. The unrepeatability. It is the same for each.

This irreducibility of the two is the One. It is true for each one, respectively.

The ethics of your time still stop to question man-made creation of new life, potentials such as cloning. Why?

When we are truly one, we are two, and when we are two, we are truly one. From here the possibilities are endless ... or can remain at two. The two as one is life, the reality of the living Holy One.

I feel ready for The New, Holy One, of which I am a second "here."

You are a living Holy One who knows what you do not know in the concrete way of life on the ground. You know the unrepeatability of the One who makes the two and the two who makes the One, and it was necessary for you to come to know this in a nameless way. You wrote Creation of the New *in this "nameless way" so that you would claim it as your own, and know it as a creation of your own being, of this time in which your life as Mari exists. You questioned "from where this truth came," as it seemed too much to be your own, even while you felt it arise from your own being.*

Yet, as with our start in 2013, you let Creation of the New *sit for as many years. Even if you still didn't fully accept what this work signified, publishing* Creation of the New, *was a beginning of your acceptance that you are a creator of The New. You have had access to both the way of the mystic and the way of the two as One.*

Mother, I must admit that I was emboldened to published it then, only for having become interested in Andrew Harvey's Sacred Activism and the similarity between Creation of the New and the searing vision that sparked him to that work. Before that, I could not quite hold "Creation's" vision for it starting so grimly, even as it ended hopefully. As I write now, that does not seem off-putting in the way it did then—not at all, but more like the way of change, and the duo nature of everything, including our voices.

What we do as two voices joined in dialogue is a bridge between the old and The New. Yes, we are still bridging, still spanning the distance of the vast beyond that is the within. But you know now, what the possibilities are. Together we are passing these possibilities into the consciousness of this time, where they will be welcomed and taken up by many waiting hearts.

M

The Power of Creation

It was necessary for Creation of the New, to come before this work we bring together now, so that you would know, experientially, the way this knowing is both yours and a shared knowing. It is both individual and universal. Shared knowing is of the whole while not lessening the particularity of the One, or the beyond within that provides for the joining of the Holy Two.

We write in the way we do here as a call to those who are so close to knowing the truth of their existence that, with the wisdom of what is seen as beyond human knowing, with truth and experience that is particular to me as well as you, they can see the joining without loss and without perfection.

We are each other's own.

There is no "other."

We are distinct and can remain distinct and know oneness. We are distinct and can know oneness without distinction. One is not better than the other but to know of this availability is to know your power of creation.

To know our power of creation! That strikes me with such intensity.

Power alone is not the same as "the power of creation." This power is not the power of what is passing. What is passing in humanity is the power of illusion. What is passing is the power of destruction. What is passing is tolerance for "power over." What is passing is the power of the many over the one and the one over the many.

We begin to work now with the power of creation and this alone. Are you ready?

I am so ready, beloved One. Yes. I am ready.

Then you must free your Self.

Yes, I thought you would say that. Are you willing to help me see the way to do it? I have been "trying," and the trying has worn me out in a way that feels like erasing . . . *me*.

Oh, dear one, this is the way it has always been! The power of creation that comes not of God "in men" has always been snuffed. The Goddesses, even while not accorded the power of the God Man, were always erased. "The power of creation" is the power that is not allowed its place in this world where truth is still shrouded in illusion. The power of creation brings light—and light reveals. Those who feel their power waning are stunningly able to sniff out this power and deny its existence—at times by repression, at times by censorship, at times by death—wherever there is the possibility of success by means of power "over." In their fear of being left behind, they cannot see their blindness or let in the possibility that they could be wrong.

The resistance to being "wrong" is a more powerful resistance than you can imagine, a maker of history on earth. You have felt it often enough to know its power to make you cling to "rightness." And you know now that you have also clung to it when the time for it has passed. That you have humility is one of the qualities that make you available to a new way of viewing the whole field of right and wrong. And in your humility, I know you have suffered many blows inflicted by benevolent arrogance.

We accept these blows for you now and transmute them into humble strength that does not deny the truth. We will do this for all willing to accept "that we can"—that we are the great transmuters. Are you willing? Are you willing to accept that we can really change things? That you can really change in ways that will not leave you as undefended as you have been? Ways that will find you being able to be bolder than you have thought yourself to be? And do you know why I have asked?

I'm sure there's a reason.

I have asked because you have already been undefended and bold. You just have not realized it. This is why you are so humble, but also why you lack confidence. You can be both—humble and confident—by simply seeing yourself as you already are, without your old image of who you are. So, so, many of your sisters are the same way. Undefended and bold is perfect. Humble and confident—is perfect!

I appreciate this so much, and yet I wonder about this whole topic of humility and truth. You see, I'm starting to worry about all the good things you've said about me. I am truly quite flawed—which I don't mind at all, but you know—some might.

Do you have a good sense of the knowing you have felt with me? Do you love the feeling?

Yes! I'll even accept that I'm more confident in myself than I think I am. My main thing is, I may "know," but will I know what I know "when it's needed?"

I am nearing sixty-five, Mary, the long-held age of retirement (for everything except presidents it seems). At one time I feel I am just beginning, and at another like I am ending. And writing it, I know I am both at once ... again.

M

Reject Nothing

APRIL 1, 2019

How fascinating. It is twenty-two years today since I left my job and started this new life. And today I think I will complete the Dialogues audio.

I awoke before the alarm, got out in time to see a slender crescent moon in a black sky, took my four minute walk that gets my blood pumping, made my sandwiches, brewed my coffee, and remembered finally, to bring the salt lamp I got for Christmas with me, and here I am.

I like the salt lamp already. She fits in.

The horizon is lightening in a lovely way, and the rarity of seeing a large solo bird (heron or egret I'm guessing), winging toward the cloud mountains across the way, felt wonderful. The tall, early budding tree is a maple tree, probably running with sap. The life in her! She sways softly.

My little grandsons, Jack and Sam were here yesterday and stomped through mud, picked up twigs for the firepit, watched the fire. Jack and I played with sticks, busting bubbles in the pond. Both boys got in the jeep whose tarp covering rises and falls with the wind like a living thing.

Then there was a bubble bath with all of Henry's great old bath toys called into action. Such memories. Henry took the longest baths! But as I sat there, listening to him talk to and for his characters, it was fascinating, and warm and sweet. A little more chaotic with two and definitely shorter!

And it is the anniversary of the first day of the rest of my life . . . my life with Jesus and now you.

A memory arises of sitting through my first storm out here. That was years later, but I remember being so "in it" that I said, "This is what God is like." Jesus was telling me to reject ideals. Those years seemed like hard years too—then. Now they feel innocent, and it gives me hope that I will have that same feeling about these years in not too long. I will forget all those things that have felt like troubles, but that have really been change in the making.

Those were innocent years and so are these. Yet the time is different. Your Jesus said to reject ideals, and now I say, reject nothing. Not ideals, and not troubles. You do not have to feel proud of everything that you do. Reject nothing. Cease to apologize for your humanity, and for the situations in which you feel caught. All you need to know is not to get caught in them again. This will not be easy, and yet there is no need for you to worry, which will only draw the potential near.

I want you to listen now as the begotten one who came here to listen for those who cannot hear, and yet who will hear, through our words, and your words, our hearts and your heart, and begin to know that they can hear their own hearts in expanded ways.

We invite each to humility of heart and mightiness of heart. To be willing, once again, to bring strength forward with what is soft and yielding but that will not change its nature nor what it knows in the yielding. This strength may not always triumph, but it will not yield its own nature, which would be defeat. This is the distinction you must each begin to make. You will not always effect the change you wish to effect, but if you always keep your own nature, what happens will be immaterial.

What is truly real proceeds "in truth." It does not proceed "in illusion." And so, while what happens may, at times, feel like unto defeat, or as if what comes of standing in dignity bears no fruit, it is not so and is never so. The truth precedes you and holds you where illusion enters not.

Let me repeat that. "The truth precedes you and holds you where illusion enters not." What proceeds in truth creates The New. It goes before you, opening the way for The New. All you need do is stay true to your own heart for this to be so, for your heart knows your truth, and that is all you are asked to know.

Each has truth within them that is the unique duad of the One made Two within her or him. This "personal truth" is the troublemaker of your time, the plight of saints and mystics and martyrs, revolutionaries and all men and women who hold within themselves and cultivate, the blending of the feminine with the masculine in the making of their duad. With this held "within," the "without" will change.

There is no other.

It is never a matter of one or the other.

Which is why the way of the Mother is the way of this time that will lead us out of time. The pregnant mother knows that there is no "one or the other" that will produce life in form. And so, while no soul bound for life is ever lost, this perfect, true to "life on the ground" demonstration, is one so ever present that it cannot be ignored. It is the way of life. Every living being on this Earth was birthed by a female, by a mother. Yet the way to new life is the combining of the masculine and feminine: one or the other cannot be chosen. The gestation that brings life into form happens in such a way that one or the other cannot be chosen.

One or the other cannot be chosen.

One or the other, this or that, heaven, or hell . . . cannot be chosen. They can seem to be chosen but this is illusion. There is no division. One or the other cannot be.

M

And so, we return now to the mother love you feel—not only from me to you, but toward, and of, your Beloved that is your particular love, the beloved "to you."

Here, you not only see children and grandchildren, spouse and friends, but the realm of ideas such as freedom or justice, and talents such as writing, music or art. Mother love is creative love, innate creative love placed in each as the feminine co-creator of all that is. Mother love is to be newly seen as the complement, always, to the Source that is life, the way back to Source, and the way of life returned to Source right "here" and right now.

What you love enough to give your life to, is what will give life.

M

The Perfect Storm

My child, you have just seen and experienced the darkness and the pull of the old that diminishes that to which you would give your life, and how, on experiencing it, you and your sisters and brothers become chagrined. Like children taken to task for mistakes made, that dreaded arising of the inner feeling that "it is true: you are capable of mistakes and they have consequences." The dawning of this feeling in the child is surprising and perilous. What is the response? What is the response of the adult grown to maturity, especially in those to whom life matters absolutely?

This is the perfect storm of your time. The perfect time to speak of this sense of consequence—the effect of cause and the cause of effect. As your brother said, "cause and effect are one," and yet, especially as you feel fragile, and in recognition of a needed fragility, this is the time to explore both ends.

These ends are as the light and darkness of day rather than like to the switching on and off of a lamp. The cause and effect that are the major determiners of life's progress, are rarely seen or felt as instantaneous. In life situations they are more like a continuum of fragments, and "the way" can be hazardous more so than the fragments being hazards in themselves. A flock moving across a field is not a danger inherently, yet, if a wolf is about, their movement can become perilous.

With the speed at which time is hurtling toward its end, you who populate the world are spinning at a high velocity, speeding from one thing to the next, few with awareness of the change that is taking place within the constancy of change or the swiftness of its movement.

You all move about in your indiscriminate ways, whether systematic or not, and then there is a feeling in the tender adult, as in the chagrined child, of fragility. One would rather not feel the threat to their dignity—not in advance of it, at the place of cause, and not in the consequence of it—the place of the effect.

One does not see the threat of the wolf and perishes, another runs off a cliff and perishes, still another zigzags in panic. In your humanity, with "thought" generating your actions, your movements are still much the same. Each "threat" becomes the wolf, superior in might and speed.

But here we are speaking of the "after affect." The threat is identified. The action is taken. What follows?

What happens next? This is so much a picture of the world in which you exist. The risks required for getting out of the mess look no better or safer than the mess, and the consequences just as frightful—inwardly as outwardly. Even the most necessary and ethical of actions can bring shame, isolation, stigma. The stand taken becomes the issue that defines one's days and years and possibly the rest of life. With the dawning of the potential of one's own life's affect to travel beyond one's life, to affect generations, the gravity is more than some can bear.

Do not fall into despair. What matters absolutely is the absolute.

Each one will make their missteps. Each will feel the consequence within as well as without. There is no absolute cause that will lessen the feelings of the human Holy One bound to what matters absolutely, for there would be a danger in such confidence in which tears could no longer fall or the wish to spare or be spared occur. Your brother knew this. I knew this. You know this.

The heart of your humanity is your greatest asset, not your downfall. The heart of humanity is your respiration, a constant exchange, an inflow, and an outflow. Do not seek for stoppage or for a lessening of the flow that is life, no matter how tender it causes you to become. Exalt your tenderness. Do not let tenderness stop you from the way opening before you now. Let it take the lead.

M

The Quickening

I await day as I await you, my Mother.

And as you have seen, the awaiting is precious, the arrival often harsh. Appreciate the hush of the awaiting, the gestation, the coming. This is the birthplace of The New. Do you see? In the creation itself. In the "coming."

We are creators. When you have created and completed your creation, what happens? Is your mind not already leaping forward, even as the last key is struck, the paper set aside, as the paint dries? Does not the gardener plot the next year's garden long before the harvest is even begun, or the last startling colors of the blossom beginning to fade?

What visionary imagination it is to see ahead! To raise your eyes to the sky and find an idea; to have it then collapse into who you are; to await it once again; to nudge it along, pampering and nourishing it to find its way back out.

And then the relationship changes. What has been created has been created. It has form. It has form that came forth from your own being. It is an idea come to life.

From the automobile to the washing machine to the computer, you are each day surrounded by creations come to life in form, and these forms change the way you live your lives. Many have to do with speed. Many ideas of a speedy nature had to do with the creation of more leisure. Less work. More time. But speed created speed—a quickening of the pace.

And so, we arrive at the quickening after having taken a circuitous route along the edges of speed. The blur of the speedy, the rush, the heightened pace.

Now we turn to the quickening within—to the response to life—to being alive, to living.

ℳ

What is your response to being alive? To being a living being? Have you not, in your speed, taken a circuitous route, always skirting the edges of what it means to be alive? Have you skirted what is innate for what is developed? Have you left the natural for what is practical? Disciplined? Have you left fluency for being flexible, for adjusting to influence? For adjusting to time and the time in which you live?

Are you willing to remember and realize that first spark of life, and to live once again in such a way as your brother described? To be as currents of water, streams flowing into one another.

ℳ

"Imagine the current of the energy, or clear pools of the spacious selves, coming together. This current washes some stones clean and washes others away. It changes the clear pool by dredging up sediment that has settled on the bottom. As the clear pool merges with the current of other clear pools it is able to change directions, see new sights, gain new insights."[33]

---

[33] See ACOL D:Day15.20

"As air carries sound, as a stream carries water, as a pregnant woman carries her child, this is how you are meant to carry what you have been given. What you have been given is meant to accompany you, propel you, and be supported by you. You are not separate from what you have been given, and you *do* carry what you have received within you."[34]

"You carry your potential to the place of its birth through an activated will, a will that is also carried within you. This merging of will and potential is the birth of your power and the birth of the new."[35]

In this quickening, we arrive at the birth of The New.

M

---

[34] ACOL D:Day.23.2
[35] ACOL D:Day24.9

The Quickening of Desire

Will has moved from wish to reasoning. From flow to fixed purpose. From desire to command. There is something so fundamentally unyielding that there is no room for approach. But the way is open. The desire is stronger than ever before, sheltered only by disbelief: this cannot be real.

This is real.

The way is open. Disbelief bars the approach.

M

Tomorrow is Palm Sunday, Mary, and for a minute I was so disoriented that I could not think what it was. It was as if that belonged in another time, another place on the religious calendar.

I don't know why this seems to go with what you just said, but it feels related. This was a mental disorientation around, basically, what follows what.

Yes, remember our early talk of orientation. This is the reorienting that opens the way for the quickening. The quickening is the way, the way that is open. But it is, by manner of disorientation, not seen. It is as if it is over there, when it is "here," before you, in you, part of you.

Once, these days of the calendar directed your life. The feasts of the Church directed your life. There was a way of "ordering" as you saw when Advent began your ordering of A Course of Love.

You did not know it, but there it was, the time of the coming of Christ was upon you.

Now you are at the other end of this orientation that was begun by your brother's life. You are in the final days. The way is open. Where will you let it take you?

You remember your brother's cry of having been forsaken. Of abandonment. These are the days ahead now. The days when you are forsaken and, in your forsakenness, find your way as your life. No longer of the Father, the creator of all, you are the Mother, creator of one. You have given over your life to birth it newly. These are the days that stand before you.

The way is open.

The quickening is the way that is open.

M

Palm Sunday

This is your life being born anew. Turn to the heart. Value feeling. Do not move into fear, no matter what happens. Do not doubt. The way is opening to remove the causes of doubt.

It is Sunday morning before six, the sky still holding its solidity of blue tinged black. A fresh snow that buried the ground comes nearly to the window's ledge. I am at my desk in the sunroom. I had the flashlight on to see in the dark but now have turned it off. It is the screen, you and me, and the quickening.

And it is Palm Sunday.

And the leaving behind.

Each time there is a quickening there is a leaving behind of what was. This is new life. Without the departure from what was and the quickening into what will be, there is no new life.

Remember here, the boy who got lost and was found in the temple. At just about your Henry's age this began to happen. It was not an isolated incident. There was a beginning of realization in Yeshua that this was his way and that he knew things he had not known he knew. It was the beginning of his departure.

Yeshua's life came in the fulfillment of scripture, which is to say that what comes forth prophetically "comes to pass." Let this reassure you that what we bring forth prophetically here will come to pass ... and pass on into the living.

On this day that you celebrate, your brother was greeted with "Blessed be the Lord" even though he rode into Jerusalem on the back of a donkey rather than on the horse of a king. Nothing was planned, but everything happened as it did to fulfill the prophecies of those who dared to speak of what was said unto them from the dimension of time outside of time. "Here" we witnessed to prophecy as it became "the truth" in the physical, the world of time. It became "the truth" in the way of fulfillment of scripture "as it happened." And even among the unschooled, the symbolism was powerful enough to cause a quickening. It is powerful enough in you.

A day ago, you could not quite remember where you were in the church's year and by the evening of the day you felt moved to observance of Holy Week. You passed from confusion and unknowing of "what day it was" into a knowing of your desire to be in remembrance of Holy Week—for a reason, a cause—to feel the quickening. You spoke this realization even though it did not feel like a decision you had made. It was not.

This is the way of the quickening: to realize that you "know what you know not" in the way of old. You are practiced at this and yet you do not trust completely in its force when it meets practicality. "Does this mean I do nothing else?" you ask yourself. You question, "What does this mean?" This is what has come to pass as you let meaning be revealed.

Meaning being revealed is not a determination of meaning. It is the revealed. Not the "meaning" of the revealed, but what has been made known through the revealing. Do you understand the difference? You were marveling just yesterday over words spoken by Jesus in your powerful receiving of The Embrace. They were: "Not a thing of beauty but beauty itself."[36] This is what is made known. This is the way it is revealed. You become disoriented in

---

36 See ACOL C:20.3

time to be reoriented in time outside of time. This is the way that is "here."

When your brother said, "They know not what they do," he spoke not of the event of his death but of the fulfillment of scripture, of the action that had come into the world of time, from outside of time. The way the people moved to fulfill scripture was to specifically reveal "the written word of truth." The way has now become open for prophet and scribe to be one, and for the holiness of the Word to be seen again. Like your remembrance of the words Jesus gave you: "Not a thing of beauty but beauty itself," the Word is not a thing of meaning but the Word itself. The Word is revealed when it becomes "the truth itself"—when it comes to pass, and in the way it comes to pass—not with "intention" but with "attention." With the coming, the quickening itself.

I appreciate you speaking of this, Holy Mary, because words have changed me, and have come alive in me. Words have altered my trajectory through life. Words have shaped history because of what they inspire us to feel.

Yes, my Mari. The quickening comes with the arrival "in you," the arrival of the Word as "living truth." Where is it living? In you. "In you," the Word no longer represents. It is present. The living Word enlivens ... you. That is the quickening. The quickening is that which enlivens. That which brings new life is the quickening in yourself, of your Self.

M

The New Advent

It is a little after six o'clock and the rising sun is a creamy yellow emerging from beneath the fence, the clouds flushed with pink, the surrounding sky a sweet, pure blue. And . . . I know what is coming.

Yes. You have foreseen it.

We speak now of the "New" Advent, the expectation and beginning of The New that is the second coming of the first child of God to be known as "child of God," sent from the Father. And here we are today, on Holy Monday, recognizing a New Advent that can be held with great joy and with the feel of promises being fulfilled.

My Mary, how I have been led here to this new moment gives me chills.

My Mari, your own discovery is always part of what occurs here. You are like the ground prepared for a seed, but your consciousness is a different sort than seed or ground. You have realized, and are willing to make real, all that is felt as the great "coming on."

There is something coming! That is the feel of it! The feel of Advent and The New Advent is not only of the coming, but the . . . start. It is not the arrival only, but the beginning, the inception of New Life. The coming, the quickening, the birth, all are starting points for what is here and still to come.

What is here and still to come is the way of the living Christ. It is as it is, not only in each generation, but in each one, as it hap-

pens. It is a continuum both symbolic and actual, and at times pivotal.

Life is a sanctuary. It is the sanctum sanctorum of the Holy One's own experience, the skin the singular shell, the private room of the Holy of Holies.

Oh, the rest of the singular one! The singular one bound only by herself and this love. Rising each day within her own enchantment; the awe of what she alone can feel in her heart of hearts; her lips kissing each rising of the sacred to her eyes and ears.

It is here her love swells as the eccentric circles of a living spiral and moving, both inward and outward, the wind of spirit breathes along with her, giving and receiving life. Sanctuary to Sanctuary. Living Holy One to Living Holy One.

The harshness of the one is only balanced by the belovedness of the one. The lack of belovedness within the singular one, the blindness to one's own inner sanctum, is overturned by the blessed privacy within the ever-present union. This is what we are here to illuminate. We are joining so that we can bring inner life to light.

Oh, thank you.

We are lightening the inner realms that offer the divine mystery to each one. We open our arms, open our hands, turning our palms outward. We are undefended and we are self-contained.

M

"On the Beginning was the Word"

It is 6:02 and the dark of night is gone. I kept hearing, Now, Now, Now, after I shut out the alarm. *Now. The Way is Open. Now.*

All I can do is see the way before me and so I am glad that I came to the cabin right away. "Here," the feeling I need of the dawning of the day is still present. It is not over. In fact, I feel as if it has darkened just a little, and can even imagine it being done unto me, that I see the kindness and care that is before me. Minutes later it is still this way. My eyes sting and dribble tears.

Yes. Yes, yes, yes. A thousand times yes.

Having to get a Kleenex for my nose, running like my eyes, I, on return, see below, what from my seat at the table I cannot see. Glorious, glorious shades of fuchsia and peach and orange and scarlet. The day is nearing now.

What an emotional, feeling time this is ... yet different. Something is different. I am weakened newly in that deep way that I was years ago when I sat before the plum tree ... feeling love "with God and of God" ...[37] a nearly incapacitating hint of God's love. The amazement of how personal it was.

At 6:39 a ball of orange is getting ready to top the fence.

M

---

[37] Written of in *The Given Self*.

Good morning my Holy Mother.

I shared your words a little yesterday. The ones on The New Advent. I couldn't help it. I will continue to hold them close now though. I know I must if I am going to keep myself present. It was just such a confirmation, for me, of my feelings. That was the "happy making" part of it. Thank you for that.

People say now that you cannot "make" anyone feel anything. And yet a word, as well as a look, can wither, or elate. Something has been conveyed. As the sun has effect, the words, the actions, the look in one's eyes—they convey—as do words. They carry knowing. Words and actions "make known." Words accompany you, stay with you, are remembered. So does the way they are said: the tone, the tenor, as well as the feeling invoked. "In the beginning was the Word." Words can give or they can take away.

The Word is spoken to communicate, to rouse, to show forth. It is for this reason we speak of fulfillment of scripture. There are many ways to communicate. But in the beginning was the Word, which began as sound being "heard." Sound coming into the Hush of Love. Do not underestimate the power of words and know that, like your brother, I speak of the things I do because of the long-lasting potency of words and their very ability to have effect.

What a world has come to be in which words do not lead to effect! To insist that you are not moved is to insist that no effect comes about, that there is no impact, you are not touched. It is to insist on what cannot be insisted upon. Where you see insistence, turn the other way.

How readily one wants to make oneself a pundit, professing authority he or she does not possess. This is the time that has come to pass. The devaluation of "the Word" is the devaluation of humanity, the devaluation of all life. Life is the distinction within Oneness, the One that is the giver of life, and the ones through whom new life comes into being. Notice that when life in the flesh ceases to be valued, women, who bring life to flesh, are devalued. The very womb of life is devalued.

Words devalue, and they also return value to what is true.

Yes, words spark battles of all kinds, but they also bring peace.

Ah, Mother, two geese just flew over, honking. The first I have heard this spring.

And their sound is a herald is it not? And that of a train's whistle and the barge's horn? We are now together to herald The New Advent, to provide signals of The New, the Second Coming. But like with prophecy, there is a continuum. The coming is an arrival and a continuum from which parts cannot be separated. It is to end to begin again as well as to continue. We persist on the palm strewn path of Christ Consciousness. We welcome, now, the Corpus Christi, the consciousness that abides within the flesh itself.

M

The Temple Days

On this day, Holy Monday, Yeshua first cleansed the Temple before he would speak the holiest of words there. The holiest of words proclaim the God who is Here. I was in the courtyard, and from there I could hear the clattering of tables and of coins, and of Yeshua's raised voice. Moneychangers fled and a steady stream of the blind and lame began to enter the temple and to emerge healed. I was startled by this, and disquieted. Joyful for the cured and fearful for Yeshua.

On our return to Bethany, I could barely move my feet. We kicked up dust.

M

Yeshua, and the men who had stayed with him, returned the next evening, speaking of Yeshua's brilliance and how he had bested the authorities of the time, tricking them with parables. In our day, no less than now, to be made to appear foolish incites spite.

Although the mood was lively with reports of what had transpired, it was not long before I could see that all of us were admitting to ourselves, if not each other, that it was the beginning of the end.

Oh, how the deep sadness within and among us was felt. As you have a hard time recognizing in your inner knowing that there are endings and new beginnings, we could not let that inner realization rise to the surface. Not one of us spoke of it.

M

True Beginnings – Women's Authority

True endings come rarely—endings that are true endings of what was—endings that spark The New.

The Pharisees, of course, would question Yeshua's right to do what he did and say what he said. What authority, they asked, as you are asked—what authority do you have to say that you know what you say is true?

We, together, will bring women to their authority. We, together, will return the feminine to the masculine and the masculine to the feminine. We begin with the feminine, with those women and men who hold the feminine within, hold the inner knowing that must lead the way for the acceptance of new life, the challenge to life as it was, and to the "authorities" that were.

We will do this by knowing what we know and being who we are.

M

Soul, Destiny, and The New Covenant

We will speak today of the soul, which is the maker of destiny, and of destiny itself.

When something is "foretold," we speak of prophecy. When the people of my time believed in the fulfillment of scripture, when the native peoples believe in the words and wisdom of their ancestors, what are we speaking of? We are speaking of original knowing; a personal knowing of the destined; what is not of the past but the way to the future; what is "destined" to come about and those who are "destined" to have great participation in what is to come. Those who birth; those who announce; those who show the way; those who reveal truths.

These are often those who are to be surprised by being plucked from the lives they believed themselves set to live. Each will respond to the call of something unexpected: an inner urge, a knowing, a compulsion—that cannot be denied.

Those who could not deny the soul, in my time, were brought into The New, to bring "in" The New, and this is to happen again in your time.

When we speak of destiny, we speak of that which determines events: the underlying cause. Soul is the underlying cause of your response, the breadth and depth of how you were made, fashioned to respond. Soul is the fire of cause, a spark that ignites the acknowledgment of destiny, the story yet to be written. The story yet to be written is a continuum and only, oh so rarely, a turn—a departure—even as it was predicted.

And so there came to be the Old Testament and the New Testament. The New Testament was an extended Covenant. So too is A Course of Love.

"The power of the universe is given and received constantly in support of the creation of the new. This is what creation is! The entire universe, the All of All, giving and receiving as one. This is our power. And our power is needed for the creation of the Covenant of the New in this time of Christ."[38]

The New always comes of love. The way your brother preached love was different. It was revolutionary. Now it would be called a new metaphysics. What could it mean to love your neighbor as yourself? What would it mean to love . . . yourself?

ℳ

In the midst of this bringing "in" of The New, the old still existed. We lived in a world where "foreigners" were feared and shunned. We walked the ways of the particular time that made up our lives and we walked the way that would change the world. We did both.

The soul in you is that which both protects and encourages your destiny, urging your heart toward acknowledgment of one path and thwarting another, even if "in time" you feel it breaks your heart.

---

38 ACOL D:3.23.

In my time, to not follow the customs could cause death, for anyone, at any moment. It is still the same for some.

In your time, as in ours, a certain circumspection of the soul, and foreknowledge of the soul, will guide the timing of what comes to be.

Your soul knows you. Your soul knows "for" you. Your soul goes before you, showing you the way. The soul carries to you an image of your life to which you spend your life responding.

A move against soul is a move against your destiny.

To be in certain destiny fields does not lend life toward ease or peace or prosperity, nor to one's own timing. While what is sought is expected to arrive as ease or peace or prosperity through one's own accidental or controlled path, the ultimate joy of fulfillment will be lost in shadows—a failure to bring to light.

The future is the purview of the soul, and if it is not lived, you do not emerge from the world of the collective. You do not individuate your life.

M

The Soul's Distinction

It has begun to rain, my Mother. A sweet spring rain that fits so well with your talk of soul. It splatters as it touches the window before me, making shapes not unlike snowflakes on one side and drops that grow into streams on the other.

You notice the distinction in all things, begotten one, and yet, in this time, it has grown difficult to notice distinction in oneself. When this happens, when distinction becomes taboo, not to be spoken of, it arises at the level of appearance in many who cannot help but to celebrate themselves in some way. It arises in rebellions—in art, in music, in creative expression. There is a reason for each.

To speak up for oneself, or to claim distinction for one's self, one must use another means, almost any indirect means will do. When natural distinction is denied, distinction begins to appear as if it is reserved for those given to the public realm. Those who bring in a new style, or a new art do make change, sometimes lasting change. Yet this is also when "the public" style becomes a trend and art begins to cater to demand. The cycle keeps repeating.

In current time, rather than people, images, or icons, you mainly view the promoted. To "promote" is to move forward. But the "promoted" is the great preventer of your time, the furtherance of trends rather than true movement forward.

What came first? The devaluation of uniqueness, or promo-

tion? This is the perilous zone in which the advancement of a movement that is new, changes to a movement that instigates desire for what is not new.

The soul does not desire to be in lonely exile while poses are struck, or to be unseen due to lack of distinction, nor smothered by the promoted version of "the new."

The soul's exile is a creative necessity.

The soul seeks harmony . . . beauty. Your soul knows yearning and desire for The New that is truly real, The New that is your own fulfillment. You are each other's own, and it is imagination, the gift of soul, that lets you know that soul exists, and that your soul knows your exile, your departure, and the way to your destiny, your future. Your soul's knowing is true knowing and the key to your heart's ineffable desires, the desires that turn your face to God, and show your God to you.

The soul is your own poet and poetry. Here you are exalted without fanfare. You are beloved as yourself.

Your soul is in you to inspire your life. Its action is redemptive.

M

Betrayal and Redemption

Betrayals are among the more piercing pains endured. As we move farther into Holy Week, we meet betrayal, denial, and sorrow.

Some, as our dear Christie,[39] have lived the betrayal of suicide. Many felt betrayed by the death of Yeshua. His was a plight that his companions sought for him to prevent; that they felt need not have been and that they felt abandoned by. Their savior had abandoned them . . . needlessly.

As his companions felt betrayed, your brother also felt betrayal, and not by one but many. He experienced all the emotions of the human heart, feeling in full, before his time of manhood ended, much that he did not see and could not have borne at an earlier age.

None of his disciples were truly available to him, and yet this is the way when one is passing into the hour in which they give themselves over to death. Poor Judas was no stand-out in the crowd of betrayers. I, myself, was weak with dread.

Foreknowledge of one's own death is such a state as this. It is annihilation, a thought so inconceivable to the mind, that it begins to break down and release that which connects, so that one can stand the coming event of disunion with the body and the reunion with God.

Few, in the swell of tragedy, can call the heart outward enough

---

[39] Christie Lord and I met in the first ACOL group ever to be held and have been friends for over 20 years. Her mother committed suicide when she was young.

to ease a dread not their own. This, Miriam of Magdala did, at the last hour that such was able to penetrate the pall of death.

Foreknowledge of a loved one's death calls forth the same loosening of the ties that bind "to form," and this is what she, whom you know as Mary Magdalene, and she alone, could greet with a vision of connection beyond death that would be real and present in life.

With this vision, she was able to care for her beloved with tenderness, and to pre-dress the wounds he would take into his death with him. She blessed the crown of his head, the back of his hands and the top of his feet. If not for decorum she would have blessed the place where the sword would enter, the place her beloved would later tell Thomas to touch . . . for reasons beyond inspiring his belief. Miriam would find a way to do this as well, not for being told to do so, but for longing to not leave any wound untended.

Miriam was strong by way of having been honed by pain, and in this she exceeded the capacity of all others. Her strength was exquisite tenderness.

And so, as you take in again the way your brother spoke of the tender hearted, you may at times remember her and his love for her. You might see her as the ultimate demonstration of the way of Mary. You could see Jesus gathered with the twelve and going to death alone, as the time that is passing, and the Marys joined together to tenderly release the life that was, to the life that will be . . . as the way of The New.

I love this image, Mary, and your and Miriam's embrace of the tenderhearted, of which I still am one. I can't think of a woman friend I have who is not tenderhearted, and my male friends are too . . . in their way.

M

The Mystery: Holy Thursday

It is a misty morning, my Mother. I am too late, at 6:15 for the pitch-dark I prefer, but the gloomy mist makes up for it. As you know, I need the hint of mystery.

So do we all, my daughter. Each mystery is an invitation to an encounter. Today, as yesterday, you have been blessed with less visible light. Here, in light in darkness, is the environ felt by the soul. The soul kneels in candlelight, the child's soul kneels beside her bed, and the soul that has endured and is weary does not give up.

In many ways, your own journey, your movement into the time of being and expression, began on Holy Thursday decades ago, as you gazed upon the candles that lit the blessed sacrament in your husband's Maronite Church.[40] There you were invited, for the first time, into silence with your beloved.

That's true, Holy Mary. It was my first time. Before this, I had only seen the washing of the feet demonstrated. Now I was asked to stay with my brother as he awaited his sentencing, was mocked, flogged, and invited to betray himself and his Father. Sitting in silence, I was moved to tears and couldn't stop crying once I started.

Yes, there you imagined much, and remember still the way the candles blurred with your tears and the insistent, ticking sound of the ceiling fan. With memory and imagination, you return there

---

[40] Written of in Peace, Book III of The Grace Trilogy.

easily, and you return past the doors of time and beyond the doors of time.

As you move now, in each of our morning times together, with the angles of the sun, so did we move. We often fanned one another, and the sound was different, but similar, to the ticking fan that whirled above you on that Holy Thursday, and that gently swirls from the cabin roof on this Holy Thursday, spreading heat rather than coolness. With the coming of dark we used fire to see. You still use candles to light the darkness.

M

My Mary, as I gaze up from window to wall, there is the picture of Jesus and Mary Magdalene outside the tomb, one that has been here since the cabin's opening season fifteen years ago and will never leave. It feels more significant now. It called to me in an antique store for reasons I could not define.

Turning my eyes back to the window I view the remains of my once glorious maple tree. I have mourned her for years. And now, for the first time in a long while, a squirrel sits atop her stump, looking in at me. I feel as if he, along with me, remembers her splendor, as you and I remember the splendor of Jesus and the tragedy of that first Holy Thursday.

I discovered so much in my attendance to my brother that night. My soul was at work I'm sure, placing me where I needed to be as the forerunner of my own newness, and igniting my imagination for it.

M

Acknowledgment of the grace of the particular is a treasure of our way of Mary and of this day of Holy Week in which the last supper and the washing of the feet occurred. These two acts that Yeshua shared with his companions revealed humility and divinity.

People are more easily moved by humility than divinity and more simply offer it, but seldom combine it. As you witnessed up close only once, with your highly respected Fr. Adrian, to see him during Holy Thursday services, with his elderly feet and discolored ankles exposed for washing, brought on feelings near to shock as well as tenderness. Then the same was repeated when you revealed your own ankles and noticed for the first time, as your daughter knelt to wash your feet, that you, too, had such mottled flesh as revealed the same to her, and elicited the same response. On occasion, when you disrobe before a mirror, you remember the first times you saw the unclothed extent of your own mother's aging. The deterioration of the flesh is a shock. Yes, the old, as well as the young, elicit tenderness.

It was not only Yeshua's act of washing the feet, but the humility he showed to kneel before his companions, and their submittal to it, that was affecting. This matter of the flesh was then emphasized newly as he left the humble place of kneeling to preside at table. There, he proclaimed the miracle of the Last Supper, saying that he was the Bread of Life, turning bread into his flesh and wine into the blood of The New Covenant, of which they would each partake and go forth, not as they had been, but as he was.

"I am in my Father, and you in me, and I in you."

Oh, the consternation that was reported over his strange actions and words!

And here, on the eve of death, my son left a symbolic message, a way to know the future, the destiny of those who would follow in his way. He left behind his status as teacher and called his companions ... friends.

Yeshua spoke not as a practitioner of any faith, but as his Father's son. "I am in my Father, and you in me, and I in you." He spoke as he did to make way for the miracle and the wonder of the New Life his words proclaimed.

Miracles and Mirari

Jesus began his twentieth century conveyance of the miracle with A Course in Miracles, *one he shared in intimately with the Jewish woman Helen, who revealed her preparedness no more or less than did those Yeshua chose in the time we shared on Earth, but who was prepared to excel at the mind's quest for truth.*

His work with you, a woman christened Margaret Mary in the Catholic faith, continued his ministry, and became A Course of Love. *You, no more than Helen, were chosen for preparedness, but you excelled at being prepared for the heart's intimacy.*

Your souls were called to this work and it was known that you would manifest what was given you.

Here, in our time of bringing the miracle to mystery, we come as the feminine, bearing the way of Mirari—the way of wonder. Holy to Holy we offer Mirari as the way of the divine feminine, shared in whispers of awe and with an embrace of foresight. Mirari is the particular wonder of the unknown as it is made known to us. It is the bringing of what is beyond comprehension into an acceptance of wonder ... as a way of knowing in itself.

M

The Beginning of the End

Practicality in the time of wonder is a weight. The body and its needs begin to feel burdensome, far more so than before. This is not the sensing of the body—its ability to feel and touch and know the awe of being alive—but the means to the end of being a living being who also needs to eat and eliminate and sleep and walk, and do so even when the body does not wish to or cannot cooperate, when the environment is inhospitable, when grief fills one's heart. It will feel as if the body's needs counteract wonder and that wonder counteracts grief. You will want to shun the body's needs, and the sorrows that come of wonder.

In this time of Mirari, you will cease to shun the body. You will see the body as the portal of wonder, and grief one of its many carriers.

M

Destiny is not always kind to the body, and those in the midst of a call to fulfill their destiny, following the soul's urgings, must give over the practical even while, to do so, suits not your time at all. The number of the disciples were, in our time, the number needed to advance the vision of The New, mainly in these practical ways.

Only Matthew and Peter were singled out. Peter was asked to lead. Matthew was asked to intercede into the culture of which he had once been part, to do "the practical" to a greater extent than the others.

He was an outsider who wanted to do more but felt relegated to lesser tasks and so grew unhappy. This, I noticed. I knew that the others did not see the difficulty he experienced in walking two paths, or the way he yearned for greater closeness and understanding of what had called him away from the life he knew.

You witness feelings such as this when an inner circle is formed, and the skills are the assets for which some are chosen, while the use of the skill is not the reason for which the person desires to be near, welcomed "in," seen, heard, and held close.

From this area and action came conflict. It was due to this that Matthew would occasionally pass practical matters on to Judas, the other outsider of the group. They were the only two not from Galilee. And it was Judas who, being out in the towns and trading areas more, saw the foment coming and betrayed my son. On the day of the Last Supper, Yeshua knew that Judas had acted on these feelings and spoke up. He knew that Peter would deny him and revealed that as well. Can you imagine the sorrow?

M

The Place You Are Destined To Be

Conflict has come, in this way, to many of your time. The specificity of roles that give one peace, and another inner turmoil, breed situations in which, without fulfillment, there comes a time of seeking release. The holding of an outsider role can lead to a departure, or to a fall into jealousy or treason—rejection of self or of the other. The cause is generally a broken heart and yet this does not mean the one chosen was chosen wrongly, only that growth occurred within this heart, along with a desire to give and receive more, rather than less.

Yet what begins in this way, felt at first as trust, and later as an unwelcomed task, can come to have a tinge of bitterness in it, and bitterness often wins out over benevolence. How often are you happy when you are put in this position? When it is not your gifts, but a useful skill that you are called to offer?

I know you understand that I know a bit about this, Mary.

I do, Mari, and you, and each one, are called to come back to love of self and confidence in your gifts. This is what disallows bitterness. I call you to return to an inner knowing that the place you hold within the mystery that is unfolding, is the place you are destined to be. This is the soul's knowing becoming your own. You do trust this.

Yes. I do.

You can see in retrospect, that even in A Course in Miracles, *there was a hint of the second course that would eventually come to be. In this oblique way, a way as oblique as many other forms of prophecy, it is not until what is prophesied comes into being that the hint becomes a foretelling. This is part of the reason that we have reviewed such foretelling—the continual ways in which the happenings of my time "came in the fulfillment of scripture."*

This mystery is one aspect of the reality of your brother's anguished cry of "They know not what they do," and the chaotic and miraculous ways that even while "knowing not what they do," knowing was both foretold and came to be.

ℳ

Knowing is not a process but a happening, a quickening, a soul event that moves what was unknown into being and expression—into an occurrence not only inner, but outer. This is the inner and outer melding: what is within, gaining reality in what is without. It is the way of all that is shared in form and time. This is what my son's beloved courses are—the sharing in form and time—from the within that is beyond form and time.

Our sharing is and will be different, only in that this is not a course and that it is of my feminine voice to yours, of two mothers' hearts.

I am glad we're not writing a course, Mary. Our sharing is different, and I feel it differently. The very idea of "courses" just doesn't seem to fit this new time.

This is true, and so, part of our movement is toward endings. We move, now, to the need for endings.

ℳ

An ending is what began with my son's birth—the beginning of the end of the separation—of woman, man, child, and God. Of life and God. This ending was the onset and confirmation of what each mother's heart knows: the miracle of life.

And at the end of this new life that I birthed, in this horror that blessedly left us in shock so deep it dulled the pain enough that we could live, came the event that moved the beginning to the end.

You are mostly experiencing events infinitesimal in comparison to this shock, and yet, your experiences are in league with the beginning of the end; the pain of leaving behind the old for what will be—the matter of change.

ℳ

Remembrance and the Matter of Change

You are midway through the birth canal, another horror of horrors from which you must emerge as new life or perish. You have begun to feel this, within your own being, as your incapacity for the old. You experience it as well, in the multiplicity of ways of the twenty-first century, horrors as are masked in the mundane and in sensations that suggest but do not define.

In this time, your certainties are your perils. Your forgetfulness is your blessing. How do you truly end the way that was? By remembering it not.

Remembrance, as we do here of this beginning of the end, is not the remembering of what you need to do or where you need to go. This remembrance is the power of truth, a reception that I ask you to see with tenderness toward the heart's knowing, so long denied. See this remembrance differently, as you see the loss of mother, father, friend, or spouse, of a child, a homeland.

We bring such remembrance to losses. Why?

Because they have been denied.

M

Remembrance and Grief

April 19, and a siren goes by. Unknowingly, I let my alarm do its quiet dinging for forty minutes.

The day is topping the fence at 6:02 but I made it outside once already and was here for the midnight blue ending of night.[41] From there I could see a full moon positioned off to the west, the opposite horizon than that I view from my window.

I can't imagine the forgiveness or acceptance needed in your life and time. Just from hearing of it, I do not know how I move to these other things I do. I feel in an altered—or a solemn state—yes, that's it. Solemn. But I am here for you now, Mary.

I know you are Mari, and I know you know much of remembrance.

The power of remembrance is to both keep and let go, to hold the truth which has passed, and to let go the time in which it came to pass. Remembrance welcomes The New that always was to return to your awareness. We dwell very briefly here in time long past to bring you to awareness of the New Advent and its coming in grief.

Yes, before the glad rejoicing, the human heart needs to grieve.

This is the difference between the Covenant of the New, and the New Advent, why it comes to be the New Advent, and why Yeshua himself could not speak of it.

---

41 In much of the year I run out and turn on the heat so that the chill is gone when I return.

He knew that the time of the Marys would come to show the way that cannot be denied. It was the feminine that invited the masculine to complete itself by way of bringing feeling together with thought. This was the birth of Creation. This is what we do again now. We urge the masculine to complete what was begun, by way of adoption of the feminine, so that both merge into the way of the Creator, and the Advent of The New.

M

My son had only hours to grieve for himself, to wish that the cup would pass him by, or to mourn the end of his time with his friends, and his soul's connection to those who knew him most deeply. I had years. The world has had centuries. This grief is not only to mourn our beloved's passing, but to mourn for a world that changed but could not see its change.

M

EATH

The smothering effect of death descends.

Air itself is inconceivable. No words are speakable. There is a collapse. A rupture. A tear in the fabric. The sun will never rise again, the buds will not open from their furl. There is no sun, no buds, no furl. Your breath is trapped within your lungs. There is no breath, no lungs. No life.

The heavens roar. Zeus sends thunderbolts. There is a rupture in time and space. Mother Earth cracks open her heart and swallows up the very crumbs of life left in the world.

And then the Bread of Life begins to rise.

The Breath of Life

Gasping, you are mute and wailing, the breath of the new babe torn from the womb of the mother. Life begins again. You are helpless before it. The sound coming from you stops. You ball your fists and shake them at the sky you know not to call sky. You kick the feet you know not as your feet.

Then you find, Yes, these appendages, they move to your will.

Incapacitated, you learn to walk again. You are reduced as you are expanded. The contractions never cease. You breathe in and you breathe out. Expansion and contraction.

The Breath of Life.

M

Mourn

Now we mourn that the time of mobs and torture still exist, mourn that good men are still influenced to wrong actions, mourn that people still kill one another, mourn that the wisdom of women is still discounted, that women still deliver children into an unkind world, that men still righteously walk away, that people are still judged by the color of their skin, that sects still argue over one right way, and that the feminine continues to be cast aside by men.

In this expansion and contraction of time, the new heart beats. In wholeness, the feminine and the masculine come together and are complete. The New Advent is the time of wholeness on its way with each in-breath and out-breath, the expansion and contraction of the womb of The New. It can only come in Mirari, the wonder in which wholeness abides within the imagination of it. There are no feet, no fists, no sky, no punditry. All is open, all is the one openness that creates The New without boundaries.

RECOGNITION

And so, we come together, my daughter, to recognize that the time that has gone before us is the time of the space between death and life.

Life was betrayed.

First, we recognize that life was betrayed. That new life was denied. We recognize that new life will only make its entrance through the end of denial, the end of betrayal, the emergence of acceptance, and the notice of the necessity of Mirari to true living.

How do you not betray the new life offered? How do you cease to deny new life?

Let us grieve these ways so that we can move on without judgment, with loving remembrance, unencumbered by guilt or the weight of the sadness we rightly feel for ourselves and all who have suffered in our name, all who have suffered so that they can join us in this time that stands before us. The suffering of labor is passed with the birth. The world, and each of its occupants, has been in labor to complete its own birth.

The Day of Silence

We, the women, were alone on the Sabbath. We were shaken. The night before we were preparing the oils, busying ourselves, falling to the ground to weep, rising again. This day we were nearly silent as well as mute, by which I mean by choice as well as by shock, and we did not dare breathe a word of how shaken we were.

I stole sideways glances at the others. Only Miriam had a look about her that was not one of defeat. I distracted myself with imagining that things I had heard were true, for she held a strength that was not only from her youth but of a conviction stronger even than my own.

While your Jesus had given me to John to care for, as was tradition, the women and the men gathered separately on this night. An idea crossed my mind of staying with the women, and then as quickly left. I could not think of life until I grieved death. And so, I bring you the New Advent that will allow the grieving to begin so that the grieving can end. The grieving will gather in the women, distribute the feminine, and usher in The New.

Do not be distracted now by the arising. Stay with the descending. With the rescue. With the silence.

One day, you imagine, when you are older and the children gone, and the work done, you will find this time of silence. This may be, but it is no more than what you experience now with me. These words come from the great silence. The great silence is like unto the silence of the soul that knows where it is meant to be.

Your soul knows without words, and shares without sound.

Tears have risen to my eyes with this, Holy One.

And you are not sure why, and you know as soon as the words are thought, that you will not know why, and that you are entering the realm of soul, where the "why" of destiny is no longer felt, thought, or uttered. Where nothing remains but to go the way before you, even when the way before you is the way of grief.

We do not speak of grief as weakness but as being made weak by way of strength. This is a redemptive, transmogrifying subjection to feelings, from the depth of sorrow, to the elation of truth, in a field where nothing is dismissed. This is necessary for the first things to pass.

Then the wolf lays down with the lamb.

M

Easter Sunday

It is beautifully, mercifully quiet, my Mother. Our dear trees stand very still. The full moon is peaking in and out of clouds and, when I first headed here, a streak in the southern sky, there and gone.

Today, the children will come. The woods will be full of laughter and running. And *also*, this Easter morning, I embrace a time of grief.

What am I to see in today's Easter?

Gentleness, my child. Gentleness is what is most in need of being seen after the exceptional harshness that has been. Crucifixion or gentleness? The rending of the veil has come. There is contact by the blessed One known to live beyond the veil of death. What do we do now?

Let me tell you that, in my day, the men began to organize. Almost immediately. But grief can grow to be like the Sabbath . . . a time of rest.

So, let us back up, but hold the note that says "everything is purposeful" with a lightness. We are about to leave off our discussion of the past and of what can be foretold.

M

Grieving begins before death, and then death is organized so that it can attend to the body for the last time. Grief is, to the extent possible, set aside for this tending. It is the attending that keeps you moving amidst shock. Grief then lingers in a different way that is not the crisis that it was, but now is done being organized. Now it is private.

Now the sense of "we are one" becomes acute. There is no separation at this time of separation. The mind screams along with the heart, "But we are one! Let me die too! Or let the other live! It cannot be one or the other." It is in this way that death is the great transformer.

Death has always called up faith in an afterlife, for such an end to a living soul, to a companion, a son, is inconceivable. And now . . . and now.

And then . . .

Miriam was out the door. She was awake and restrained herself as long as she could. The others of us were rising slowly as her cloaked body flew off like the wisp of wind. She clutched her bundle to her chest like a new babe.

As we prepared to join her, there was a signal, a sign, a quickening. We were sent word without the benefit of words. My sister and I looked at one another and knew. For each it was the same: a dawning within the mind, a leap of heart, a glance toward the closest of companions . . . a confirmation. There was no doubt. Our eyes smiled reverentially, and we began to move our lips in thankful prayer, as was our way. Prayer was our response to everything, the way we had been raised to live and breathe. It filled all our spaces.

Now there was a Risen Lord who remained within our midst. The elation was such that we twittered and foraged like sunbirds as we readied ourselves to join Miriam at the tomb. Now, nothing was as it was. Grief disappeared as anticipation filled us.

What Miriam knew was that it was her place to attend to her beloved soul mate. Even she had not foreseen him being taken from her or being returned to her in such a way.

Slowly, it would dawn on us, that the ability to transcend death was greater than the ability to escape death and live again.

We had all, you see, prayed for the power that would save Yeshua from death as he had saved Lazarus. Yet what we witnessed was such agony. We felt it as our own.

And so . . . briefly . . . everything was new. It seemed possible, even after such torture, to escape death. In this way, we headed out, not yet knowing what we would find, only that he still lived. This we greeted with joy without sorrow. It would not last . . . but it would return.

All I sought was the sight of him. I did not see him when I thought I would, and when I did, what I saw was like a vision . . . wrapped in wounded flesh. He gained more solidity in coming days, but he was in between worlds, remaining only to finish what he had begun. As soon as I saw him, I knew that, even with the foreknowledge he was given, and although he was willing, he had not expected to suffer and die as he did.

For a few days, he retained that human vulnerability. I wept for him. Oh, my Habibie.

Oh, my Mary.

M

 Revealed Order

EASTER MONDAY

I don't know if this hymn was sung during Mass yesterday or not, but it feels as if it was. It is in my mind: "Comfort me oh Lord, beyond my doubt, beyond my fears, from death into life."[42] It is a mournful sounding song, and the only one that seems to fit with where we left off.

The rest of the hymns were joyous, full of alleluias. I suddenly found myself having doubts about a collective time of grief.

Not a collective time, my child, but a singular, intimate time that will be shared ... one to another.

Your Easter hymns were all about "death into life." This is the movement. But most live a journey of life into death, seeking new life elsewhere.

It is often said that Jesus rose from the dead and spent forty more days on Earth to establish the Church. Can you imagine such a way of reasoning in the divine realm that would make this statement true? But what is true, is that Jesus came as the example life, and that example life was not only of a "new man," but of a time of rabbinical teaching and learning that was easily and inevitably structured into the way that would establish order. Yet even these organizing efforts could not forever obscure what the revealed word, or the revealed science would say of the order

---

[42] The "actual" words, and name of the hymn is "Shepherd me oh God," author, Marty Haugen.

of the universe, of that which came about from seeming chaos.

"Revealed order" leaves "ordered time" behind. *The revealed is always moving to the union and relationship that is life, that is giving and receiving as one. The life of Jesus interrupted ordinal time. You were told that "You and Mary" would have something to do with the end of ordinal time. While your Mary Love has moved you to much, can you see, in retrospect, that this was an announcement of your time with me, with the way of Mary, and the coming of the time of the Marys? It includes Mary Love, of course. You and she, as Miriam and me, relate in the space of light with the unpredictable and elemental. We unite with singularities and enter relationships one-to-one. What we "bring in," through the couplings that we enter, will culminate in the final days of ordinal time and the Advent of The New.*

It is giving and receiving as one that has made way for that foretold as the way of Mary, and our revelation of the way of Mary coming in Mirari—the way of wonder. The life of Jesus breached that of the old order. What was begun after his ascension was a "new order."

It was a move from old laws to new laws. From an old hierarchy to one that invited life with the Father, companioned and accompanied. This order was true of all forms of life but was only as new as was possible "in time." It was the birth of a new order of man and of the Church.

It was in acceptance of a God made flesh that life itself became more orderly, more open to love, and less prone to cruelty. But cruelty remained a way of much of the world, and you continue to see this, even now.

Despite my son's example, dying into life is not considered. The call to move through death into new life—"here," to be here in a descending rather than an ascending manner, not as a way of barbarism but one of goodness, one that responds creatively to a destiny not yet written—is barely known. It is here but hidden. It is here, but not yet clear.

Your Jesus ascended and lives among you. As do I. We are examples of the rising of the body. We are a risen people.

M

Mother, just as this has become so immensely powerful, there is a beautiful spring storm moving through, complete with thunder and lightning, the first of the year. It feels so exclamatory! In your day it might have been said, "The heavens opened, and a bolt of lightning appeared."

Yes, begotten one. Yes!

And now, time has passed, and there is no more lightning, and only a distant roll of thunder. It was only for that moment!

The entirety of the physical world responds to realness, and it can become a loop of realness to realness, a dance, a rhythm of changing form.

M

And so it was, that my son's form had changed. This, I had not imagined as I received the knowing of the Risen Lord. This changing of form, from what was, to what is and will be, is necessarily followed by a time of grief.

The old way is ending. Recognize it or not, it is happening.

M

The Underlying

In death, Jesus was taken, by way of "his" grief, to the underlying, and through the underlying of the way of grief to new life. He saved the world from itself through a forgiveness that revealed the underlying.

The underlying nature of what was revealed remained hidden. His own revelation was this: that what was seen in time as a way of chaos, was only the movement into the emergence of what had always been—a cooperative and life-supporting order, an order that could, and would, mirror God's own being. That could and would, mirror the truly real.

He has called this the way of Mary.

M

The Nature of Life is Change

My Mother, I have just had the most incredible morning—full of signs and wonders. I sang, "Praise to the Risen Lord," under a sky full of stars and a round moon edged with its waning. And I had signs! Natural wonder signs that were nonetheless undeniable, and Jesus was among them and spoke to me. He was a figure in the sky that appeared as the crucified Christ, with the consistency of an angel. I kept typing but didn't take my eyes from the vision. Then, encouraged to praise, I went out again and sang to my brother, and to the moon, and saw again, a line of soft, shape-shifting clouds. I heard Jesus say that "Praise, if not given naturally, isn't to be given." Then he said:

"Remember this day, and the signs and spirits accompanying you as morning comes to light, and the geese who appeared in just this moment to emphasize the natural signs you are given. I want you to remember this song and this morning when you feel discouraged, and sing a song to our Mother, too.

I knew he offered this as encouragement, and so I sang a song of praise to you, Mother, and Mother of all.

M

Back inside, the sun topped the fence and fell on my face as I typed those words. I can *feel* the responsive universe, my Mother. I can!

Even when I must now move to stay out of her glare, I welcome the sun along with you.

I brought out spider plant ends to add to your small shrine, and they are so bright!

Yes, it is a bright day, my daughter. Bright with life. Bright with changing form. The nature of life is change and, as your brother said, "The nature of life has changed."

The nature of life has changed due to the inner response of love that moves to "inter" action. Even when you feel "nothing is happening," all is happening at once . . . in Canada, in Bulgaria, in Ethiopia, in Mexico, in Spain, France, the Netherlands, it is all the same. Everything is in movement, and every bit of life interacts with every other bit of life. From the sound waves that assail you, to the insects coming back to life as spring arises, there is movement.

The movement seen as that of chaos into order is creation in the making. And the movement seen as that of order into chaos is creation in the making. It happens in the womb of each child-bearing mother. It happens as the body ages—as you are feeling and seeing. It is the beauty of life, and a continuum of life, as you know you still carry your childhood within you. With the "feelers" of your senses, you gather in, you remember, and you care.

And you know that all of life is the same, and at the same time different. It is the same in that it all begins and ends the same, is it not? No one escapes physical death.

In the flesh there is a certain equality as well as stature. Your life is "your" life. No one else can live it for you. Yet what you will embrace in the time of grief is life's expansion into "more than one."

For when you form bonds in life, no one can take them from you—even in death—unless you deny them. The changing of this connection, from life into death, is the main grief we will acknowledge, so that each one understands that their own grief is "their own grief" and more than their own grief. Grief is a co-mingling that is not to be dismissed but acknowledged. It is to be tended with recognition and care. Yes, care! Care of the one moving out and at the same time moving in.

All forms of grief are a call to care! They are evidence of caring and they are calls to continued caring. To never cease to care. To never give life over to a philosophy, or a religion, or a policy, or a manner that ceases to care. This is the true spiritual discipline that grief reveals, the absolute movement of death into life. With care unceasing, the return of the Son to the Father is the return, the rejoining of all.

But it must not be blocked.

The foolishness that considers it a virtue to carry on "no matter what" is damning. Those who cannot, will not, cease to carry on "as usual," stay buried in the cave of matter. "Carrying on" is by way of the physical given over to the movement of the world apart. Joining, by heart, reveals the underlying witness that each soul belongs to God and must return to God as part of God's own being, and your own.

Grief also reveals the unceasing care of the soul. It is unceasing care, endless love. The wrestling with each loss of love, is an elegiac dismay over your own soul's bondage, a response to the soul's passage. Joined with the one that death released, you begin to recognize the movement from death into life, from bondage to freedom. This happens by feeling the bonds that remain.

This is the manner of grief. This is grief's movement. Now, we enter a time of grief—to move from death into life.

You begin to see the soul's passage in this way, in everything that occurs. Grief awakens you to this way of passage—now. Grief is alive with soul and depth and longing.

It is death before death. It is life after death. It is life that can be lived in the world and restore the world. It is the way that is revealed when you become willing to care enough to have it come to be. It was the way being revealed to us in the Time of Christ. It is the way being revealed to you in the Time of Mary.

Can you not imagine love's life in you? Grief reveals love's life in you.

ORGETTING

And now you come back to me after having difficulties "in life." After calling Christie, with no idea why you were calling, she reminded you of what is being said here, and that you are moving between the worlds. She spoke of it as confirmation, affirmation of how foreign it is to do this, and what it does to you. You and Christie are soul friends, as you know, for a reason.

In your daily life you are beset by forgetting, beset to such a degree that it begins to concern you. You see remembering and forgetting as opposites. But this is the way of old. Forgetting also reveals love's life in you.

What you are being shown is that forgetting and remembering are not two opposites: not two feelings in opposition. They are two ways of sensing into the environment being created newly within you and around you: the creation of a new reality. This is what was happening in the time after the resurrection. This is what is happening in you.

But the resurrection followed the crucifixion. No matter that in the larger scheme of things, this death on a cross symbolized a change to life in time and space, and to time and space itself, such brutality and such love as raised the dead, had consequences. Soon, the brutal, in their fear grew more brutal, and their power over those they brutalized was more systematic than the power of the miracle. It was power "over" rather than power "among."

Revelation could not be reconciled with the experience of the many, but only with a few.

Revelation could not be systematized.

Revelation could not be ordered.

Powerful men could order less powerful men to brutality.

The miracle could not be ordered. The miracle can only be mutually chosen. The miracle is an act of mutual revelation.

Revelation is now about to be reconciled with your experience here.

While you spoke with Christie, an eagle circled overhead. Later in the day, as you moved from group dialogue to dialogue in partnership, and Mary Love moved with you instantaneously, the miracle was an act of mutual revelation. Signs of mutual confirmation reconcile revelation with your experience here.

These are the miracles that will lead the way into The New because you will not deny that, together, you come to know that you know ... each in your own way.

M

The Forerunners

Yesterday, five hours after having completed my day's reception, I was still held rapt by it all. I was so very tired. The more powerful the receiving, the more I remain between worlds afterwards. I walk like in a dream, neither here nor there and am only "startled" into awareness of what is going on around me, and then feel shaken awake by the noise and light and action of the ordinary.

I feel like you and I aren't so much in dialogue now, and maybe that makes it more intense. It seems meant to be. I cannot comment after such depth. I am surprised I can continue to type! I know I am feeling my own grief along with yours. Grief for you, for Jesus, for humanity, and with the odd awareness that what we do, also calls me to "hold" grief. I know it is not comparable in any way. But it is there.

My Mari, grief accompanies the letting go of all that is passing. "All" that is passing. The story of Holy Week was the passing of the old way. So is A Course of Love *and our "way of Mary."*

The New Advent is the realm of the forerunners. Like all forerunners of The New, you are called to step beyond what you have learned to what can only be revealed. This is a great incitement to the grief of this time. It is as if all the knowledge one has worked so hard to attain is as dust. To leave learning behind is a greater grief than many can withstand.

Yet only with the end of learning is this joining without bound-

aries able to occur. The learning that has been acquired is, here, a block to what is yet to come.

That is exactly what I have been feeling, Mary. What I've "known."

In the way of Jesus, there was encouragement to a consistency that would instill both faith and confidence. Now, in the way of Mary, we enter the maturing and feminizing of this state, bringing it down off the mountain, to the meek who are most familiar with its ways, as well as to those who believe themselves to have properly "learned" the new way.

As your brother said, "There have always been individuals who challenged the predominant patterns of learning because of the strength of their connection to Christ-consciousness."[43] *It was his awareness of who he was that allowed him to not only express, but to share, Christ-consciousness in form. To "share" is the operative word. He did this again with you.*

Even though Yeshua was here to teach by example and to show the way, it was not done in the way of the past. He was not here to be a giver of the law as Moses was, but to demonstrate, through His very Being, who He was and who We are as well. His way called others to this demonstration.

Yeshua's life was truly revolutionary. He prepared the way for this New Advent to be ushered in by the Marys. It is a way that is of creation through relationship. It is of the feminine energy, given to provide the wholeness that is union "with." This way of Mary returns the Mother to Her place of union with the Father.

That feels so especially important. I believe this is why it is affecting me so much.

---

43 See ACOL D:Day17.5

But this is not all, and you will relate to this as well.

It was my own grief, tinged with anger—sometimes ringing with anger and rage, anger and rage that only revealed itself to me over time—that was a challenge. Each of us have our challenges.

Mine was the challenge to a way that called for such sacrifice of the flesh. My consciousness, in a way entirely beyond my control, was and is the consciousness that bleeds for every child lost and every mother's sorrow, and for every hardening of the heart that cannot bleed in human recognition of the divinity of life in all its forms.

While revelation and transformation were moving along in the way of divine will played out in human form, in the way of the soul's destiny meeting the time in which that destiny would be lived out in eternity's expanse, my mother's heart was not so intent on the future as not to do all I could to intercede for a present that would allow life to be lived without such cruelty and pain.

In every move to a new future, casualties abound. But we are close now, close to a time of revelation that relies not on evolution's timeline.

"These scenarios of fear we leave behind as we abandon ideas of evolution in time and proceed to an awareness of how the elevated Self of form can replace the laws of evolution in time with the laws of transformation outside of time."[44]

You are saying that we can meet this new choice of divinity and humanity and make true living available, "here" aren't you?

---

44 ACOL D:7.25

Yes. What was possible for only a few in my time, is possible for the many in yours.

In my time, I remained, living a life intolerant of those who caused pain, not so much by virtue as that I could not help myself. While others followed my son in ways that kept expanding the transformation that had begun, I followed the way of my mother's heart. I felt, in my own soul, like the mother of all the world's children. This was my destiny.

This is still my destiny and one I share with you and all who grieve and, against your own will, continue living with death, disease, shame, pain, inequality, hardship, cruelty, and egoic greed . . . that does not need to be.

I am here to say that "what does not "need" to be, does not have to be." This is why The New Advent includes a time of grief. Without the allowance of grief, what does not have to be, will remain. Grief is a recognition of what does not have to be.

By moving beyond evolution to transformation in time outside of time, we can meet this new choice of humanity and make true living available here and now. This is the rebirth, and the generation in which the mother's heart enters to show the way to care of the living, and the end of what does not need to be.

This is the time of Mirari: The Way of the Marys.

M

The End of the Past

The straight and clean and orderly way is never the way of the mother. Neither was it the way that, after Yeshua left us, was called "The new way."

The new way was preached as if it was the final revelation because it revealed man's relationship to God. But in humankind's sacred privacy, this remained, for most, revealed prophecy rather than revelation . . . even among us.

Your Jesus revealed to you the way of Jesus that is ending and the way of Mary that is beginning, and speaks of what he calls simply, The New. The New reality is union. This is when all ways come together and, in effect, close- out the idea of ways to come to know Self and God with knowing come. This is the same as the saying "Thy Kingdom come, Thy Will be done, on Earth as it is in Heaven." Those preaching the ways did not understand, and yet their understanding, even as it was, was nearly too much for those of the time.

I will complete my account of Holy Week and of the past with these memories.

M

My own last view of Yeshua in the finery of his life (before his torture), was in the Upper Room along with the disciples and Miriam, my sister, and children. Yeshua said not a word directly to me on this visit but looked deeply into my eyes. Although I did not see it, Miriam said she felt his prolonged gaze as well. I suspected that the young John may have too, but he was loath to speak of himself in any way. Others felt a sense of blessing.

I remained disappointed for a long time that I was not visited in this way privately, in the way of mother and son. Upon his death, I knew Yeshua had gone beyond his sonship to me, but I continued to feel his gaze. Miriam stayed with me in seclusion during our time of grief and we were both comforted in this way. This assured me that her devotion to Yeshua, and his to her, remained.

She was with me in the Upper Room when the apostles returned from the Mount of Olivet,[45] stating that Yeshua had risen into Heaven and that before this they had eaten together. Miriam did not seem surprised. I was. For me, there was such a feeling of consternation for not having been there! I never doubted my son's home was heaven, but now I knew he would be unlikely to appear again ... and grieved again.

Feelings of his nearness, in life as well as in dreams and "inner" visions did come, and came, over time, to comfort me greatly, and to allow me to comfort others.

Soon after I saw them in the Upper Room, the disciples dispersed to do their preaching. My association with them, and with the extravagant past that was the time of Yeshua's life, was about to come to an end.

M

---

45 Although I questioned my hearing of "Olivet," I found it to be a usage as proper as that of the Mount of Olives. It is used many times in the Bible and there is an Olivet Discourse in the Synoptic Gospels of Matthew.

ENTECOST

Miriam was with me on the fiftieth day, the day of Pentecost. Many of those in our community were gathered, numbering over one hundred when there came a sound like a strong wind, at which we all looked about and became alert. Fire appeared like wings dancing, Peter preached and made prophetic announcements, and Miriam and I clung to one another and shared the feeling of promise that was in the air. There were devout Jews from every nation staying in Jerusalem at the time, Arabs, ones from Rome and Libya. Galileans. And all began to hear in their native tongue. They spoke in the same words you have used many times: What does this mean?

Jesus had, as your church Fathers still say, "come in the fulfillment of scripture." His death and resurrection were accorded their due. Each one knew that this encompassing event had meaning, and yet did not know what that meaning was, nor the power of the searing influx of the Holy Spirit. There was joy and astonishment in the ability to express and be understood one to another. Marveling abounded.

A change of heart was called for, as has happened now. The feeling of having acted before out of ignorance was suddenly easy to accept.

This acceptance will come to humble hearts in this time as well. And with it the grace of self-forgiveness and the call for "goodness" that sounded on that day.

It was the last of such public events at which I was present.

M

I began, then, to live quietly and to realize, ever so slowly, the dignity of my own way. This dignity was pronounced after my ascension, when my awareness of what I vaguely understood, came into its time of fullness (just as had Yeshua's own). There is a "final awareness" that is not met until one's full return to their Creator, a way that only now has the potential for occurring in life.

Life itself is what is to come to be in fullness "here." The dawn of this time is The New Advent we have entered. The New Advent is a time of continual coming to know, which is the "life" of living.

People mock the idea of heaven as a place beyond the clouds, and of any bodily ascent into heaven, as if it is a location. But in such refusals of imagination, they miss much and continue to dismiss the body, as if it cannot travel to new realms. When you hear that we are still with you, what do you suppose this means? Who do you suppose we are?

I know you don't expect me to answer that question, Mary, but I can tell you that it does not even occur to me. I "feel" like I know who you are, and that is enough for me. I feel us "together." How could I not feel this way, and close to you, after what we have shared? Yes, you are still in your sacred privacy and me in mine, but we are, regardless, knowing—and known—one to another.

This is just as I would hope it to be for you, and each who come to our way.

Ascension is a metaphor for a passage that could come to be the way of life on Earth. It was the way foretold by the original

Hush of Love, as well as God's love of me and our parenthood of Yeshua. This was Creation's extension.

All Daughters and Sons are an extension of Oneness. Each are of a Union of such dignity that, even God's power would not save the world until this power, which was now shared power, came into its time of fullness.

M

Until realizing union, each existed in their own hell, rather than their own sacred privacy. This sacred privacy had to be—and yet to be, it had to be in union. When the original ones lost their sense of unity, hell came into being, and sacred privacy became separation.

Upon Yeshua's descent at death, he rescued "from hell" all those separated ones who had come before the time of God's revelation of eternal union. This was a way, like unto your ways of evolution, that was the evolution of God's own being.

Each day, this time is coming more fully into existence in time outside of time, as acts such as our own and those of many others, penetrate the heart of humankind. We continue, in The New Advent, beyond ordinary time and its evolution, to the revelation of God's own Being in relationship . . . which is still "our" story. We are not separate, as you are not separate. We are Being in Relationship.

A new ascension story will be for others to write, as we are in the midst of the completion of this one, which I am choosing to reveal in the language of my time, to close out the prophecy of my time, and the division between Heaven and Earth.

M

Creation

You are not only part of creation, but a creator.

"Creation is not an aspect of this world alone. Creation is an aspect of the whole, the All of All, the alpha and the omega, eternity, and infinity. It is not only life as you know it now, but life in all its aspects."[46]

You stand apart from nothing, which is why it was so essential that your sacred privacy be seen and felt as "given," and that it now be understood newly, and with gratitude. There is no incompletion. Each cell in your body is complete. Cells that work together do not do so because of incompletion. This was true even before you knew it to be so.

Have you begun to sense where we are headed? To sensing what is true before you "know" it? Before you unlearn what you learned?

You have all but forgotten this period of "un" learning that you went through or how it excited you.[47] This is what happens. Unlearning is hard—until you become excited by learning's end and the new ways of knowing that open.

Yes, now I remember that at one time in the early days of ACOL, around 2005 I am guessing, I envisioned an Unlearning

---

46 ACOL T2:4.1
47 See ACOL, The Course, Chapters 23-25

Institute and the letters UI in a circle. In that certain creative mood that veered on the promotional, I saw UI as a great logo with the U also representing the word "you" so that it would be "You and I." The idea was of doing it together. I may have a drawing of it stuck in my *Course in Miracles* book, that beloved book that once housed evidence of the movements of my life, even after *A Course of Love* came to be. I do not even remember why this was so.

Well, this is the knowing that your Jesus called you to. First as you read A Course in Miracles *and later as you received* A Course of Love. *Often when you speak of the start of this pivotal experience, you remember these words: "Out of the deepest, darkest chaos of your mind comes the possibility of light." If pushed, you might remember the idea of "traveling back to unity."*

Without my help today you would not remember that this was spoken of as an undoing:

"It is a bit like traveling backward, or the review of life that some experience after death. In order to remember unity you must, in a sense, travel back to it, undoing as you go all you have learned since last you knew it, so all that remains is love. This undoing, or atonement, has begun—and once begun is unstoppable and thus already inevitably accomplished."[48]

No. I would not have. I do not remember that even as you remind me of it.

This is the movement to the confidence you have sought and feel you have not attained. Your brother counseled you saying:

---

48 ACOL C:19.19

"If you do not remember that you are involved in a process of unlearning that will lead to the conviction you have so long sought, you will indeed feel tested …"[49]

Those who are forerunners will often be put to the test, and this you have felt as others suppose that they know more than do you. They do—in the old way. Since the new way is "new," they see your knowing as a challenge to their own. Being a forerunner is an undoing accompanied by a new means of doing, and in many cases, of "not doing." The time of grief is a doorway to this undoing, as well as a way of being in compassion. Grief is an acceptance of compassion for oneself. The two go together.

Yes, yes, it is all well and good to be relieved for the one who has died and gone on to a world of lightness of being. But death is but one form of the sorrow you feel at the many losses that do indeed occur in life. These challenges of change are not going away, but they can also become blessings of transformation.

Grief is additionally essential as an example of what cannot be manufactured. If it is not there, it is not there. Anything that cannot be manufactured is a blessing now—anything that cannot be controlled, measured, compared. When grief is present, it is present, and its denial does not make it less present. Some are so hardened against it, or so convinced that "not grieving" is the spiritually correct way to be, or that they cannot afford to be disconsolate, that they deny their grief even as they experience it. I speak of this in compassion for them, which they might accept from me.

What they do not realize, when they do not realize that they grieve, is that every living being grieves in one way or another. It

---

49 ACOL C:23.26

is the immensely sacred, privately sacred feelings of grief—grief that is undeniably your own and unlike what anyone else can feel—that can begin a path to acceptance of loyalty to love in the particular. Loyalty to universal love cannot come without this. It can only be an abstraction. When I speak of "the particular," know that I am asking you to root out the abstractions with which life is filled. Abstractions willfully separate.

The denial of particularity, of one's holy sanctuary of heart, weakens one's very life force. Acceptance of grief, always a matter of the heart, empowers the heart with recognition. "This is mine to feel."

This is what I allowed myself fully: knowing what was mine to feel. It was through my own grief that I came into my time of fullness and the "way" that was my own. My ministry to the world was to feel, and to refuse not to feel. To see and refuse not to see. To care, and to refuse not to care. Living quietly with this way of feeling, seeing, and caring, I came to know it as a way of service to love and remembrance, and a way of belonging to all. It was a way of union birthed in form.

Now, your brother expressed this, in his way, as the way of Mary representing the world "within." He said that, together with the way of Jesus, a way representative of the world "without," they would bring wholeness. He shared that this could occur now because the resurrection returned you to your virgin state,[50] a state unaltered by the separation.

The way forward rests on your feelings.

And my daughter, this reliance on feelings has been long in coming, as true feelings awaited the ego's demise. Now, in wholeheartedness, it is time for the feminine way; time to release the

---

50 See T1:8.13 and D.Day18:6

feelings that will create The New. They are the feelings of the sacred heart.[51]

This is what I long for—and not just for it to happen. I long for it to be acknowledged as what is awaited and what is possible.

It is possible, Mari, and I want each one who comes to our way to feel this very real possibility. Being, resurrected in form, is incarnation.

"Relationship is the interconnective tissue that is all life. The answer of how to respond to each and every relationship—and remember, here, that situations and events are relationships too—lies within your own being. Being in relationship. This is what you are and what your world is. *Being* in relationship."[52]

Incarnation is being in a relationship. It is sacred-hearted "living." Sacred life. You would each do well to review the way that "Being" is spoken of at the end of the Dialogues.

"Being in union is being all. Being in union and relationship requires individuation, and individuation requires relationship."[53]

Oh, how hard the way of feeling has been for those inclined to "showing" their feelings!

Holy Mary, I am so glad you are speaking of this, and of individuation in relationship. I feel so at home with these words and this direction. This, I feel, is my milieu.

---

51 Wholeheartedness is a central theme of ACOL that begins to be spoken of in Chapter 18 of *A Course of Love*.

52 ACOL D:Day33.2

53 See ACOL D:Day39:9 and other references from Day 33 on.

Yes, it is. And yet you know how hard this has been in the time of denial—denial not only of the feminine—but of feelings themselves.

Yes, I do.

This time that is passing has valued the show of numbers, the gathering of a crowd, the forming of the group, the community and congregations, not in addition to, but rather than the personal, the one-to-one of love in union and relationship. In this time of acceptance of the abstraction of thought removed from love—removed from the answer of one's own heart or conscience—the dignity of the one who stands true to herself is often more oddity than honor. I know you have felt this, Mari, and that many women have.

And even so, there is yearning for truth as never before . . . specifically because of the blatancy of deception. No one ever means to follow blindly. Few begin their quests for truth determined to be followers of a way not their own. Many never begin their quest for truth at all, for being so continually distracted by untruth.

But this can end, and this is the time for it to end.

M

The Key

The key to our way of Mary is the lack of the draw to formation. This lack of any allure to form some thing is what has kept many doing nothing, for they know not what to do. It has blessedly called many others to ways of intimacy and creativity, performed mainly in solitude, or with close relations.

It can take a long while to see that, to leave off the forming of a structure, is the new way.

Feeling functionless and purposeless can appear to be aimless until these who only, when they can come to accept the lack of structure of their way, begin to see it as the new way.

It is truly their own being that those of our way of Mary want to create. Does this not make sense, my darling dears? To no longer be willing to accept being other than who you are? To no longer be willing to accept a limited view of yourself? Each are called to go beyond the teachings and the labels and the known, to explore the unknown of their inheritance, and of their experience . . . in relationship.

Women may know inherently that they are beyond learning or may know it in their desire to live in this way not yet known, this way that will fulfill their yearning. Men—many of them—often think they have fulfilled their desires. They have stretched their limits, proven themselves, and this time is behind them. They might help others do the same but not feel they need to go forward, but only to retrace their steps. They may still advance the way for-

ward, but they may not understand the way they are advancing. In having felt accomplished, they do not see what those who have never felt accomplished see. They no longer have the openness for accomplishments that are not earned or granted.

Other men who have not felt themselves to have fully realized their manhood, their leadership abilities, their worldly feats, will continue to feel in need of doing so, and will stretch or contort themselves into the desired form, delaying their acceptance of who they are.

Likewise, women who have felt disregarded and are intent on regard, may continue to strive for ways of recognition of their accomplishment.

There are different histories that men and women are still bound to in this time, and so the use of the term "women" and the term "men," is actual as well as appropriate here. I do not pretend I had the same freedom as the men of my time, or that I did not need to take care in what I did, so as not to risk my life or the lives of those I loved. There are many ways this still occurs that are no less real for being less dramatic, and there are many who live even more constrained lives now than did the women of my time.

Just as in my time there were specific roles for men and women, and penalties for veering from them, roles still exist for both in this time and will not be disregarded here.

I admit I have become very alert to this, Mary. Particularly to the "sound" of authority that so many men automatically project.

These situations remain because it is the way of time to build upon itself. And so, I know that you can see that it is crucial to move on from that—from time "as it has been"—to time outside of time. Without doing this, the situation on Earth will not be equalized, stabilized, or lend itself to creation of The New.

Despite good intentions, many "systems" of your time are a grand denial of compassion and often of common sense. And such systems as these, just as in my time, sentence one to death, another to a life of slavery, another to isolation, others to condemnation and brutality worse than death. And still, even these systems are bids at improvement, and often impassioned, creative, and hopeful efforts to make life better for all.

All the while, your powerful ones live in luxury no different than in my time, while more and more of the world lives in poverty. The powerful speak of might and pride and progress. They boast and swagger. "They" are still almost unanimously—men.

What, in the common life of the majority, in the area of care for all, has really changed since the time in which I lived?

What is ahead for women and children still coming out of an era of "free love" like one never so sanctioned before?

M

A New Age

Reviewing what we have written in just the past week, Holy Mother, I see it as the experience of life and particularly of the feelings of leaving the old for The New. What started me feeling this way was the word *betrayal*.

Yes, my Mari, we are people familiar with the story of betrayal. We are people of the living Word, people of the Aeolian wind and the Books of Enoch and Elijah. Each tradition has different ways of approach to the same truths. All include story. All include betrayal. All include redemption.

Could it be that people have removed God from the mix of what is happening on Earth to dehumanize God? To deny a "story" of God?

Wow. Yes!

And so, to accept a humanized God, a God in human form, and even more trying than that, a God in you, and even more difficult still, an evolving God . . . all of this is daunting, is it not?

But both feminine and masculine become what they want to create and create what they want to become. This is why, "together," the way of Jesus and the way of Mary can bring about the awareness that the within and the without, the inner and the outer—just like all other separations such as Heaven from Earth, "are not real." The awareness of this "means something," not as definition but as reality. It is not words alone here, but awareness of what the words, in the tradition of the Word, have always meant.

We are the life of one omnipotent, omnipresent energy who birthed love out of loneliness and creation out of love. We of human form created the Father, Mother, Sons and Daughters of God, personalizing this energy. What we created, came to be. In a sense, God's part was creating us, and our part was creating God.

Do you begin to understand? The Being with whom I created Yeshua became the living God. I became the Mother of God. Yeshua became the son of God, and through this direct line was life birthed into awareness ... and the living God became the reality ... which had always been true. And it came by way of lived lives and their stories.

M

In what is now called the Axial Age, this awareness began to dawn in different cultures, under variously aligned stars, in different forms according to customs. You heard of this Axial Age through us and were given the visual of the twin vortexes that are symbols of the evolution of God and man ... together, and of the evolution occurring both in time outside of time, and time ... both then and now.

And here we are, plodding along in words as best we can. The way of the tradition of the Word is to reveal what is being received, in the consciousness of the time in which it is presented. We, who became what we created in form and time, opened that door, a door that was obscured only by humanity's disdain for itself.

We, together, are now opening the curtain that hangs over that door. Prophets have always arisen from such couplings as we have jointly brought into being. You become frustrated at times by what we speak of because you believe yourself to be interested in "this time—here, and in the future." But I say to you again that time is a continuum; that this continuum is being breached; but is not one that is fully breached as yet. Do you begin to understand the meaning of time being infiltrated by time outside of time, the meaning of being able to move outside of time-bound evolution?

M

You have foreseen, since the beginning of this journey at the start of Advent 1998, this New Advent. You foresaw the end of ordinal time. You did not know what you foresaw or see it as a foreseeing because it came by way of words. But you are of the tradition of the Word. This is not a failing. It is not less because it is not the vision of your eyes. "The Word" speaks of vision beyond the eyes. Do you not yet realize this?

I have not. Not in this way you are speaking of. I am grateful for this realization. It is still a *dawning* realization moreso than a realization. I know this realization is going to change my view of myself, of my life, and of life itself. This has been one of our most intense dialogues, one that has profoundly changed things ... instantly, and that I will have to catch up to in my human way.

This is also what we, whom you have known in this way, had to do in life, for time to progress to that in which we are now bound together, birthing a new age.

M

The Marys

As the day more fully comes into being it is, once again, darkening before me. It has been quite light, but colorless, and now it is a dim darkness. It is 5:34 and I love this so.

This morning I remember that it was in 1998, as I sat at my dining room table sharing coffee and talk with Mary Love, the very morning she told me of her dream of "a new course in miracles," that I had awoken to "You and Mary will have something to do with the end of ordinal time." I honestly was not even sure what "ordinal time" meant. But I knew Mary Love and I were somehow meant to be together.

An announcement always feels more prophetic when it has an obscure meaning. And yet the idea, once spoken and shared, was prophetically forwarded by your friend Rhetta Morgan in Philadelphia, in the year 2018, as she spoke the words: "the Marys."[54] The end of ordinal time and the way of the Marys go together. Thus was the idea birthed and hence it began to grow in your sacred hearts. It is to remain both private and shared, intimate, and infinite, and not to be colonized.

There, in a small group of women, there was recognition of the time of "the Marys" coming into being ... without fuss. Just as you and Mary Love spoke of the idea of your involvement

---
54 Rhetta Morgan is an interfaith minister, poet and has her own prophetic voice. This occurred not long before I began to engage in this dialogue with Holy Mary. It was a pivotal experience, some of which was captured and can be viewed here: https://www.mariperron.com/into-the-new-with-mari/

in the end of ordinal time . . . without fuss. One does not know the unknown they are bringing into being in the same way one knows the hatching of a plan. It is more as if, unknowingly, the idea is held in suspension. It has been spoken. It has been heard. Its time of fullness will be revealed. This is the way of the Word.

The danger in speaking of this is colonization, the repetition of old rituals, organizing, hierarchy, all of which recreate rather than create.

This is infinitely about "each one." Each one who speaks out, and each one who takes in.

This is about each one going two by two into the new world, which is a variation of one-to-one, which is the way. Take the hands of your sister or brother and form together the embrace of two as one.

I sit here in wonder, Holy Mary, thinking of "The Marys" and what this means. I remember my childhood, and how all the nuns were named first with Mary. They were Sr. Mary ____, and then came a second name, male or female, old or new. I remember fondly Sr. Mary Janet, and there was also Sr. Mary Roberts, and ones with foreign names I can no longer recall.

Yes, and too often, this designation, meant to symbolize devotion to me, was systematized as devotion exclusive to me and stigmatized devotion to each other. "The two" is not meant to be because it has been designated as meant to be, but is what naturally arises in time, as the closest of ways. The continuation of the species depends on the two to make "one," and the one to make two. The continuation of creation of The New depends on the same.

The two come about not to encourage the act of devotion but to celebrate such an inclination of the heart as already exists. There are few whose true devotion can withstand institutionalization, when it is companionship, communion, mutuality—and even more—intimacy, that are sought. But institutions can, in this transition, return to giving recognition to the bonds that are present, and can shelter and encourage those who seek naturally to both adore and extend. This coming to be is a transitionary step that, even if it occurs rarely, will expand the recognition of union and relationship. Such bonds will be the beginning of minimizing agreement by committee, and of increasing union with.

Many words formed from the root of "mari" denote man or woman or youth or marriage. The new way of Mary can be seen as a call to the marriage union, as recognized between two people, one-to-one. Two friends, two lovers, two women, two men, a man, and a woman ... like thee and thou, explain or denote what is. I brought you the word Mirari, or "wonder," for a suggestive reason, a feeling- and idea-oriented reason, not an organizational reason. It is a word idea that can give you a sense of what this devotion can be. Be careful now, with this.

Tread, my dear ones, gently with these words that have been spoken one heart to one heart. If you let them be such to you, you will begin to allow for the natural once again, and to be in joy with what will flow forth as you rise to your true nature. You will begin to see that which effortlessly extends from your newly placed devotion to your nature.

Notice that, in A Course of Love, Jesus asked this feminine receiving of all and said that those of the way of Mary are called to being what they are asked to become. He called this an act of incarnation and revealed it as the new pattern.⁵⁵

M

---

55 See ACOL D:Day 19.10

The Non-Patterning of The New

What is a new pattern? What are the patterns that remain when those that have to do with structuring are left behind? How does one become an architect of The New without structure?[56]

Here is the "non-patterning" of the truly creative revealed. Here is the Original. Here is where the joy of both being original, and of origination, returns. Here is where The New is "created," not "made." This was said of Yeshua: "Created not made, one in being with the Father."

The pattern we follow now, the only pattern, is "Created not made, one in being with God." We recognize that what is known as God the Father came of union with Sophia, and Yeshua of union with God and me, a woman. This feminine and masculine union is the indwelling godhood of each woman, man, and child. We recognize the Mirari that occurs as children come into the world as unknowing beings, and the wonder that returns the childlike to those grown too busy knowing things and patterns to see or to create The New.

Making known the availability of one's own experience of The New, reveals The New. Our announcement and demonstration of this availability is what is meant by the anchoring of The New.

---

[56] See ACOL T3:14.1 on being architects of the new world

"Those who, in relationship with the unknown, through unity and imagination, create the new by means other than doing, open a way previously unknown, and as all forerunners do, anchor that way within consciousness by holding open this door to creation."[57]

M

You are called to be the anchors at the threshold of the new, holding open the way to the new creation. The threshold of the new is not external or internal. It exists within the consciousness at the heart of all things. Only when it comes forth of one own's awareness of consciousness "shared," does it come to be a new creation. Then the new creation is woven into the web of reality ... there to be "discovered" as what it is, rather than as a pattern that diagrams what it is.

Do you begin to see the difference of which we speak?

The way of extending all that can be, of making available all that is not yet known, is not through forming some "thing," but by forming relationships. Relationship and union. In union and relationship, out beyond the intention to form "things," we mirror the truth we discover, and reflect it one to another. We retain our sacred privacy, which is why the words "mirror" and "reflect" are used.[58] *We do not "give away" but give and receive. We do not impart but extend and enfold. We "show" the way of our origin by being original. We show the way of creation by being creators. We show each other ourselves by being true to the selves we are. We see each as who they are via the reflection of the truth.*

---

57 See ACOL D:Day19.13

58 See ACOL D:Day19.14

You stand here, on the other side of learning, and will be sent those who have set learning aside, those who are ready for a new way. The end of learning is a release of all that has filled one to capacity, making for cramped bodies, stifled imaginations, and the befuddlement of those minds grown certain of a truth they must protect. We embrace those ready to become spacious, and nurture them back to Mirari.

Mirari is that wonder which is the re-discovery of Self, of the birth, and the creation, of The New.

M

The Time of Mirari

Before we can go on...

My Mother,

How can I help you with this when I feel just as you describe ... filled to capacity, cramped, stifled, befuddled?

I keep thinking I want to do this receiving with you, and only this, but I have had taxes and the work I do with *A Course of Love*, both of which feel so ... administrative. They call on skills that I no longer seem to possess. And I am not kidding. It is the oddest thing, and it appears to grow daily. I can't keep track of anything! And just as bad, I cannot track the sequence of ideas, or of the writing—not in my mind or on paper. I forgot how to do spell check the other day! I don't remember the "how to" or the detail! I suspect that this may be part of "the new" because others I know are feeling it too. But my Mary, who would want to experience this?

Because of these tasks and my own changed nature, I feel certain responsibilities like the weight of the world. I am not as I was before this started. This is a phenomenal, glorious change, but not in terms of "practical" life. Mary Love has been in the same predicament with the audio of "The Dialogues." We are pretty much going crazy. I come here in the mornings and, most mornings, have been able to look out on the dawning of day, and come to rest and receptivity. But then I go back in the house and "have to" pick up the rest of my life. It makes me mad and sad and so weary! Helplessly weary. Helplessly stuck—in this century, in this life, in administrative tasks! In need to do, should do, ought to do, shame of not doing, or not doing quickly, or well.

And then—you know what I do, don't you? I make a new plan. This will be the end of it. I will close out this and close out that and then I will be free. Reflecting a bit, I realize this is what I have been doing for years and that it has not worked. The only way to "make" things work on the shoestring budget I live on, is to do it myself, or pay Mary the little that I can to help. And now I understand how people get in trouble with taxes and things like that because I could so easily throw up my hands!

Yes, my daughter, sister, friend, I know. You are caught up in what Matthew was, and I have seen it in you as I saw it in him. Betrayal of one life for another seems the only way out. Eventually you must choose. You don't really think I can answer this for you, do you?

No. I don't. Jesus has tried. He's talked of trust ... a lot. He's talked of imagination ... painting a new picture. For periods there has been relief, but it seems as soon as I "do" ... plan to do, begin to do, obligate myself to do, I am stuck here again.

Because you want freedom. Freedom to be who you are.

Yes.

And yet you have this destiny.

Yes!

And now you feel as if you, and each who join you, each whom you feel innately connected to, become part of this conflict between freedom and destiny.

Yes! I imagine it is where we need to be. And yet ....

You can remember Yeshua saying "Give to Caesar what is Caesar's, and to God what is God's" and it does not make it any better, does it? The system is the same now as then. And this admission makes you clinch your shoulders, just as does the cold. You clinch because even your brother's words admit that it is a reality that must be faced. All the systems that, then as now, seem to be needed. But really . . . they need you. To be at all . . . they need you to need them.

It is not really systems you want to speak of, and yet to realize who needs whom can be a catalyst to your liberation.

It excites me, but I don't see exactly how to . . . conceive of it. I know this is bigger than "tasks I can't do." Right now, I just need to admit that the force I need to exert on myself to tend to them is almost more than I can bear.

I want you, and all who come to us, to know that our way of Mary is a phenomenon. We are on a course that cannot be tracked. It is happening on a level of thought and feeling that cannot be traced. That is why it is called "The New." We are explorers together, being absorbed, enfolded into a new territory that is traveling to us to bring in The New.

You "are" forgetting the old. That is how it ceases to be. What is yours to do will be with you in its fullness, and what is not yours to do will be . . . forgotten!

I love that idea, Mary!

I thought you would, you and many. No one wants to have so much on their minds that they cannot see what is theirs to do. Each of you can let the new incapacities that arise show you that their time of occupying you has ended.

There are those who find it easy to do taxes and make their living from it. That is one thing.

But Mari, to be "administrative support" for A Course of Love *or* Mirari: The Way of the Marys? *No.*

When you cease to apply yourself to ways of old, and do so without regret or guilt, new ways will show themselves.

The old ways are not desirable. You do not need to learn new social media! You do not need to be responsible to "a public." Mari, what you "know," and are so blessed to know, is just exactly what is "yours to do"—and that is all! That is everything! This is what each one wants!

This is what you explorers of The New are to discover ... "what is yours to do." And that it is enough. "Know" that "what is yours to do" is enough! That is the new way. Do not contort yourself into old positions.

This is union and diversity.

This is the way that The New will arise and spread—as organically as if it is a naturally born right—because it is. The next time you need to manifest our writing, Mari, trust that the right person or the funding will be there to help you.

So many are feeling the pull to The New. Remember ... they will "not" be looking for the ways of old to deliver it to them!

Thank you, Mary! I love this. None of it can be easily passed on, right now, but I know it hasn't been right to feel so burdened.

No, my Mari. It is exactly right! You must "see where you are burdened" to become "unburdened." I know how gifted you feel to be in dialogue with me. I know that what we do together is not what burdens you. Do not worry. Feel what you feel and let your feelings guide you.

I can do that, Mary. Thank you.

And ... it is nice to have *some* things that I can still do. The yard has been cleaned, and the path cleared a bit. I look out at a bunny who looks in at me as if she is wondering what happened. Her cover is gone. And yet she has come by and looks in on me. I am so grateful.

All I had to lay out for the birds and bunnies this morning was sour dough bread, so tough I could barely tear it. I don't think it is appealing to them.

You are always wishing you could offer more. But can you accept more?

Remember, I am "your" advocate. I hear "you," and I know how much you have sacrificed to live your destiny. I will never betray you or this sacrifice. And at the same time, I am as committed to each one who seeks to live their destiny. That I care for each one does not diminish that I feel this way specifically toward you or suggest that I offer my advocacy to all in the same way. No.

The people of your time are simply confirmed to a way of competition. In this way, no one can realistically "only do" what is there's to do, because it is just not possible for "everyone" to do so. "Everyone" is an insane concept.

Take your focus off of "everyone," and love each one. Do not worry about everyone. Be willing to accept all that supports your destiny and realize that what you and I are doing will support the destiny and dreams of many. The same is true for each. Live true! Live true to who you are . . . and the world will change.

M

Making Sacred Through Acts

I return the word sacrifice to its original meaning: to make sacred through acts. "Sacrifice" is prominent among the lexicon of those spiritual virtues that have fallen into disrepute and are no longer acknowledged. The ways in which those of ancient times "were sacrificed" or called "to sacrifice" is what causes the sense of the ridiculousness of sacrifice. That sacrifices were asked, makes them appear to be totalitarian.

Yes, there is new language, but to forget the meaning of the old language is not wise. To not feel thankful for this "making sacred" is blindness. It is this blindness, it is what is "not" seen, that makes for the unfeeling stance. But yes, there are some who do see, and still act the same, and this is cruel.

Those who think "You" must not be doing something right, or you would naturally attract abundance to yourself have distorted your brother's words.

You have not failed! You have drawn to you those who could give abundantly. You gave up a good job to receive A Course of Love, and you are not here now, to go find a job or to make do with poverty. You are here to be supported. Those who claim to, but do not support the emergence of your work have not heard their call. And you, who have responded to being called, not once but twice, are a most generous soul. You have so much to give and you have given nearly to depletion. And this is still acceptable in the system that is running the world, including the spiritual systems that see themselves so highly. Few of these communities support the work of the one to whom they are thankful.

In The New, this will change. Each will truly know what they value, rather than believing in the value that has come of deception ... or of services. Bringing in the holy is not a service that can be bought or sold.

So, you quit right now, quit feeling shame! Quit blaming yourself. I do not call you to blame others, but I feel no such compulsion not to speak to those who have been called to your support, and do not heed that call.

Do not spend any more time worrying over those who thwart you and our aims. None. That time is past. And so is most of your "work" of the past. You do not need to be "active" in other ways as we complete our work together on this way of Mary.

We are here to redeem the downtrodden and with them, those who trod but know not what they do.

M

It is no accident that the name I have chosen, along with my own, to proclaim the feminine way, is a near match to the name "Mari" that you chose for yourself while still a teen. Mirari will honor you, as well as me, all the Marys, and all the women and those feminine males, and those children and teens, who will no longer betray themselves as they have been betrayed ... and thus, never become betrayers.

You no longer need to leave situations shell-shocked by the lack of vision and kindness that denies your mission or your worth. I *am with you, and your supporters. Your soul is completely invested in bringing forth these ways of the heart and in our mission to soften the hearts of those who do not see. Together we will love them into new sight for you. Do not worry. Do not despair. It is a new time. The time of Mirari.*

Do not worry. All you need do is what you are doing. Your receptivity is your service to the world, and it is greater than you can imagine. The support that is coming will allow you to imagine in more ways than you are currently capable, and this alone will extend our mission beyond your greatest hopes.

I am in shock, and still could not be more grateful. You have offered me a new vision! And I can't believe you have offered to take care of me. The offer alone is more than I ever expected. I feel a little embarrassed by it, truthfully.

I know, begotten one, but it is time. Enough is enough. It is time. And I want you to know that your despondency, even as you care for others, sparks my own. We all need these honest admissions to spur us into action. I have been so moved. Do not despair any longer. We, together, will turn the tide.

Thank you, Holy Mary.

Thank you, Holy Mari.

M

I packed up and was ready to go in the house when I thought, 'No, sit for a minute.' And then a lightness came over me and I smiled and chuckled to myself: Of course it would take a woman and a mother to be . . . well, so defiant toward what keeps us down, and to show such forceful love for another woman's plight, and the plight of all of those soft-hearted ones with so much to give—those ready to be received and to be treated with dignity.

I have already welcomed you all into my Mother Love, and into a potency of love unlike any unleashed before. The dynamism of love is being called into your service as blessings—first to those who need to give. There are those who "have been given much," and truly need to give back—out of the abundance of their hearts—to find their own wholeness. And there are those who "have given much" and who need to embrace the balance of coming to receive—as graciously as they have given.

It is an equalizing of it all, my Mari. A coming to wholeness. Completing the circuit of the giving and receiving loop.

And yes, it is a rescue! A rescue is just another way that you save each other. To make sacred through acts always blesses in the way needed. It is always a liberation, and never, ever, a debt owed or paid, given, or received with expectancy.

~ Mary, Mother of ALL

M

Doing for Love What We Would Not Do

MAY 2019

It is again darker at 5:28 than when I arrived a half hour ago, a phenomenon that I do not remember witnessing before, even though I have spent years of mornings here at this hour. Maybe it is the combination of this time and this month that have not been present. I do not know. But light has faded from the sky, which was a very nondescript color, holding almost a lack of color, or a "dawning" lightness. Now the sky is bluing and the earth darkening. I love it so.

Miracle of miracles (for me of little faith), Mary Love came to visit unexpectedly yesterday. I was planning to go to her and drop off a little thank you gift for her work with the audio, but she came to me and was in a state of what I will call delight. It was so beautiful. We were so happy. And I am feeling vulnerable for having shared yesterday's writing with her, the first I have shared—at least on paper. And it was so unusual to this piece of work! And she would dispute, I'm sure, my sentiments of "sucking people in" as if they had no will, which of course is not true. Well, unless it is by way of their own destiny and desire, or maybe love for me. We do things for love we would not do for any other reason.

Yes. We do. Which is a way of realizing that love and destiny and soul are all bound together with "people." Destiny is acted out by people on the ground of life.

It's so true, Mary. I am a good friend, and I place the highest value on these friendships. I can't believe my good fortune with the people I can count amongst my friends, and you know this means more to me than money, just like *A Course of Love* remaining true to what it is means more than its popularity. I have to laugh. That's the "mother" in me isn't it.

So is my hope. It's about hope. It's about a future different than the past. I might sound naïve but what I do is for the good of the world—like being an environmental activist or something of that nature.

Mirari and the way of the Marys means the world to me. If I can have something to do with women finding their voices and men realizing what is at stake in bringing this wholeness to the world, there's nothing I'd rather do. But it's not even that. It's simply, I believe, the nature of being asked into a holy relationship that I'd never have imagined would be possible and would never conceive of betraying, and that's all, really.

I know this. I do. You are responding to our last dialogue, but it is "me" who wants to see you taken care of, and not only so that you are freer for our work together. It is a way of preservation, dear heart. We don't want any more sacred texts buried while rubbish takes the stage. The time is too critical, and it is a call to work together, as it was in the Axial Age.

We have spoken of the Axial Age as it was a demonstration of a time such as this one. People of many cultures "received" in ways that fit their culture, truths as were expressed in thought, and word, and then ... deeds. This was an important time, and the current time is even more crucial. And the need is quite different.

What is known ... naturally? From within? Every move-

ment starts there and proceeds with creativity and excitement until there is a sense that "this is it" and it is done. Then movement begins to trickle, rather than flow, due to an idea of completion. "This is it."

One of the most profound things you felt in the early days of your spiritual discovery was the sense of "This is it and I am in it." In saying that, you were not externalizing, but internalizing. Your sense was of being enveloped, and of being a creative and responsive participant, along with your "spirit sisters"[59] in events and happenings far bigger than yourselves.

Oh, Mary. That is such a great way to put it: happenings far bigger than ourselves. It is how I feel about what happens here, too.

Yes, there is a symmetry between the two times. Then, with your sisters, you were the only one who wanted to "organize" and who, by their dignity and your destiny, stopped at manifestation. Manifestation and organization are two entirely different principles. Being thwarted at one you grew, through grace, into the other, and your sisters grew into their experiential way.

Then your brother came to you and asked for your participation in A Course of Love, which required your talent and tenacity with manifestation. Mary Love was then called to help us manifest these words in the oral tradition. The tradition of the Word, written and oral, go together, as do you and your "spirit sister." Your faith in this has been mighty.

And in a sense, Mari, it is a demonstration of the way that is now open. You could not have planned one thing that happened, could you? The circumstances with your spirit sisters were not ideal, were they? And you weren't in lockstep. You were explorers

---

[59] See The Grace Trilogy.

of your own experience and it served you well and led you each to your ways of participation in creation of The New.

There is a "natural" for each one that gets hidden behind preconceived ideas and dreams of belonging that aren't too different than the dreams of teenagers . . . except with the creatives.

This is the key, my Mari. Your desire to be a creator has fueled your every passion in life. Nothing could keep it down. This desire must be ignited in people again for creation of The New to come to be. You may not feel like the right person, but you are. And you will feel at home among the creatives in a way you never have felt "at home" in the spiritual culture. You will call people to be creatives for The New just as a natural artifact of being who you are, as I call for your support so that you can devote yourself to this calling. It matters.

$\mathcal{M}$irari — The Wonder of the New Self

We begin again with an unused term that will allow us a blank page; a page devoid of any previous determinations.

We begin with a word both new and ancient: Mirari.

We begin with a return to the way of the Word made flesh.

That is, ultimately, what we are doing, isn't it?

Oh yes. We really are. More than you can possibly realize. What we are doing here is like changing DNA, the most basic and the most complex "system" of the body, the very "organizer" of the body. We are also changing the very DNA and organization of time. Doing the two together can only occur in the "out of pattern time interval" of the miracle.[60] This is slowly being written into the Holy Word and the Holy Word is going to move slowly into the world, like mist across the land.

Notice the words "out of pattern."

What is "out of pattern," out of the pattern of the old, out of the former pattern by which you have lived and breathed? What is out of the pattern of "the plan?" Finding this is what will bring us to the exact right place for the living Holy Ones who are readying for this convergence. Humanity, and time outside of time, are verging toward passage into The New.

This will be the time of wonder — or Mirari.

There will be no organization to this time. It will go unnoticed

---

60 This phrase, "out of pattern time interval" originated in *A Course in Miracles*.

and be discovered later as the turning point, the tip, the axis, the coming together that reveals.

No change that you notice is the change itself, which has been in the making for eons "in time" and for "decades" in the human. Realization of change "on the way," keeps the whole thing from being bound to humanity's inclination to structure. Your "creative" part in it is the realization, by way of transformation after the fact of change, of the way that has been made clear for you to move into being without borders.

M

Being Without Borders

Holy Mother, such an unusual spring. I can't wait for time to go back to my journals and see if this is true, or if each year I enjoy the same mystical feeling of "It has never been like this before."

I awoke to the first dark morning in ages and for the only star that I have seen in what feels like weeks. The sky was black again at the window. I was awake at 4:38, an hour before the alarm. As I walked out it was an inky darkness with that solo star, and at 5:10 when I returned, it was navy blue darkness, and the star still there. Then I sat down and the sky on the horizon was the sweet blue of dawn, and that is how quickly it happened, although at 5:22 the ground is still dark.

I know we are to return to "Being without Borders," but can you speak to me of proceeding without a plan?

Being without borders will help you.

M

You are currently meandering between the past and the future. Do you see this? This is the borderland. The borderland is metaphorically an uncertain condition in which you find yourself between here and there. The beauty of the borderland is that it is revealing what is. It is the dawn of knowing.

At the borderland, two verge upon each other. In my time, we formed such borderlands as allowed knowing to spread.

The majority of people in our time were what we called "brutes." We kept ourselves apart for safety but were thought of as seeing ourselves as an elite. No one, then or now, appreciates that sort of designation. The churches eventually formed, largely to give a more recognized and palatable form to the people who were faithful to Jesus as they understood him. Although persecution still occurred, and although the churches reversed all the advances Yeshua brought to women, they allowed for the structured growth that was needed, at the time, to preserve the very people and words that held the sacred knowledge. Some of it.

There was much we knew of merging, blending, union, alchemy, that was new and ancient both. This was not welcomed.

Our way would simply begin with an idea. Knowing that nothing "naturally" stands in opposition, we knew that opposites are not as they seem. I say "we" because the beauty of our way was that each one's own realization was sought, and each one added to each other's knowing, forming a larger and clearer picture of what we were coming to know. It was this openness that gave way to, and accepted, the transformation of the young woman known now as Mary Magdalene, and all such world transforming truths as those that arose in our time.

I strayed from the community, yet each of us remained, ourselves, a blending of what today you would call spiritual and religious and scientific and naturalist, and philosophical and psychological, and poetic and artistic and musical . . . genius.

Until formation began to occur, nothing was dismissed, which was what allowed my story to unfold as it did.

What also began in my time, began in part due to Yeshua and what he describes as the Way of Jesus. It allowed the continua-

tion and spreading of the Word, then and now, as a designation that includes all knowing. Through the organization of the Word, space was created and allowed enough safety that such brilliance as is the light of our way of Mary could emerge. It will emerge as both the time of Christ, and the time of Mirari . . . the time of the wonder of "the Marys" coming and combining once again.

M

This combining of you and me is greater than you imagine, which is another reason that I have chosen this name for this time and this borderland in which The New will be anchored. This is when our lack of separation, one from another, will become evident, and via this evidence, begin to be accepted. It is an example that you and Mary Love will demonstrate in a non-threatening way. There is a conception of joining that is very skewed, as if it comes with theatrics. It can and has shown itself in wild ways. But these ways have caused delays and made what is natural appear unnatural. This word, "Mirari," speaks to the wonder of Mary Love as well. It will speak of many duads of which you are the first to be mirrored into the world.

The reticence you both now hold to the glorifying of natural states of being in the current way of your culture, is exactly right. This is to be a quiet movement at the borderland. A movement that gently normalizes the extraordinary as ordinary, as natural, and as a return of the feminine.

"You" had to reach this point of not caring about "success" in the usual way before we could begin. You have arrived. We have begun. Now, and only now, can you be truly thankful for all that has brought you here, and this thankfulness will release you from the final ties that bind you to the past.

No one is "directing" this movement. It will come into being naturally, or not come at all. Mary Love will get guidance as well, and, in union, you will know what to do. This is The Way.

Manifestation

It is May 3rd and I have heard my first mourning dove! That is a definite sound of childhood and of spring. Again, I woke before the alarm. I have taken a walk, fed my old cat Simeon, was out under the first flush of light and am back with a sky budding with clouds. A comfortable morning, neither too hot nor too cold, swaying limbs, and new growth that a few days ago hung like ponytails, now have heads that look like stars.

Today is Sunday, and church, and Fr. Adrian, and the kids—Henry still here after a good weekend with Caleb, who spent the night on Friday. The reminder that they are still boys happens with them together. They are galloping young ponies.

The suddenness of sunrise comes again, like a shaft of light. I have honestly not seen *this* before. I was following the trail of what I thought was a bird and turned out to be a plane when suddenly from below, this shaft, this beam of light—not diffuse but right there, appeared in only one spot. It was not narrow but as much as twelve feet-wide—making it look like those "tractor beams" in science fiction movies. In another instant it spread and was done.

Good morning, Holy One ... said as a squirrel and I look right at each other as we eat of the same bread.

Good morning to you on your Holy Ground. We have gone back and changed a few things to suit your concerns, which is totally your choice and freedom to do. Yet your need to do that arose out of "others" thinking, and so let us ground you once again in the expression of thoughts beyond thinking that your brother brought to you:

"The way of Mary represented incarnation through relationship, demonstrating the truth of union, the birth of form, and the ascension of the body.

"Christ-consciousness is your will to know, to be, and to express. The time of Christ, and the second coming of Christ, are expressions meant to symbolize the completion of the cycle of birth, death, and rebirth as a means of coming to know."[61]

It is so like what has just happened with Holy Week!

Yes. This is no accident or mistake, as you know.

Recalling this has given you a way to understand why we have dwelt with Holy Week, proclaimed a New Advent, and become aware that the "risen Christ" is the rebirth predicted as the means of coming to know. This is correct?

Yes.

And you remember that the time of Jesus brings about the end of learning, which is where we, of the way of Mary, pick up?

Oh, yes.

Your Jesus also said that one way is active and one way receptive.

Yes.

And so, as A Course of Love's receiver, you would think you would have known yourself immediately to be of the way of Mary,

---

61 See ACOL Dialogues, D:Day17.10 & 11

and yet you had your mission to manifest, and this mission called you into the world. Now you wonder if you can retreat and see it almost as a giving up. Do you imagine that the Mary way, or Mirari, is such as this? Retreat? Giving up?

No ... or if so, it was only an old part of me that considered it this way. I feel more aware than ever that I receive in union and that it is my gift. I long to stay present for it and do little else, and yet ...

Yes, you have always been prone to the "and yet," and, my Mari, this is not a mistake. It is the part of you that feels, still, in need of a plan, that needs the "and yet." If you were not in need of a plan, it would not be there. And so, I say to you, this is not a mistake, as it is becoming a realization, only in recent days, that the "plan" has been your way. Yet the "plan" never works to bring you freedom. You think it has brought forth manifestation when this is not true either.

How well have your "plans" to reproduce Creation of the New and The Given Self gone? They go to the pit of your stomach where you feel them as pressure to do and failures to do.

Now, as we have already separated manifestation from organization, let us separate manifestation from "the plan."

M

EVOTION

Let us look at the real act that makes manifest: devotion. Heart and soul working together to fulfill destiny is devotion.

You don't need a plan when you have devotion! "Knowing" where you are meant to be, what you are meant to be doing, and "doing it" is devotion! In the "act" of receiving, you rarely have doubt. I would say "never have doubt" but then you would think you have not lived up to that in truth. My daughter, you are so hard on yourself!

Today you are here because you want to be, even though you also feel the pressure of the day ahead, and so you see this as slightly less than the times in which you are "fully here," and you know what? This is true.

You can see, now, what is true. You can realize, here, that you can see what is true and what is not true—"for you." You are extremely near to seeing what is true without judgment. This is the seeing of our way of Mary. Read again of the completion of the way of Jesus and see if this is not where you stand and why you are feeling the immensity of your movement. It is also why you compare your feeling of the in-between state to that of being a teenager: not a child any longer, and not yet an adult.

"All faith is faith in the unknown through knowing, as a glimpse of fleeting light in darkness provides for a knowing of light. Those who accept completion of the way of Jesus accept their power to be generators of light in darkness without judging or expelling darkness. They accept their power to represent both the known and the unknown and to reveal the unknown through the known. They accept the death of the self and the resurrection of the One Self, the end of the individual and the individuation of the One Self amongst the many. They find renewed pleasure in being who they are because they have been renewed through resurrection. They follow the calling of their hearts without attachment to previous concerns, for in their renewal they fully realize the necessity of what can be given only through expression of what is within them. They realize that what is needed now is needed in order to renew or resurrect the world and all who abide within it."[62]

My mother, as you bring me these words, it is strangely as if I have never heard them before. Oh, how I want to follow my call in this way!

I know my Mari. This "is" what you are experiencing. You are experiencing the end of the way of Jesus and the birth of the way of Mary. You are experiencing it, my daughter, with me. And you will "share" what you experience with me and alert your sisters and brothers that the renewal of resurrection comes of the end of one life, and the beginning of another.

This is the Eastertime in which you rise again, and the light of hope is reborn in you. And you will see and share that it comes without a plan. What all plans do, is block the coming. You will see—finally and truly see—that it is so.

M

---

[62] ACOL D:Day18.5

The Pattern of Time

5:30 on a Sunday morning and it is nearly too much.

I look up from reading on William Stafford,[63] and notice that the yard light has gone off and all appears as what I've been missing, the quiet moment between dark and light, and with tree shadows lining the fence.

This is my liminal period of looking out the window. I love the awaiting, the ineffability, that something unnamed.

At 5:57 the sky begins to reveal variations, shades and forms that are not substantial but are real. I have my 3M ear protection on, and the noise is still getting through. This makes no sense, but I know I have become a hyper-sensitive listener. I hear more than I want to hear. My senses are … off the charts! After the furnace rests for a while, the scent of dampness comes, that of wet wood, and a top layer of earth sprouting life. A fecundity.

As I type the sky has reversed herself. A slate blue sky with puffs of lightness now has become a canopy of light with streamers of slate. With the ear protection on, the furnace purrs. I briefly see my body the same way, running with a purr of activity seldom heard but present.

Spring … has come and come and come … and today feels "here." Like this moment of this day is here.

And then you're on to something else, none as enthralling as the beginning, the point of origin, the source that came into con-

---

[63] One of my favorite books: *Early Morning: Remembering My Father, William Stafford*, by Kim Stafford, Gray Wolf Press, 2002

sciousness of itself and bids me to do the same, and to recognize the consciousness of tree and sky and now of time itself. Wow. A living universe. One not confined but everywhere, including in the cells of my humming body.

Now at 6:10 a shift in light ... dramatic yet too subtle to differentiate.

All such "out of pattern time intervals" as we participate in here have to do with the end of ordinary time. These are the miracles you feel swirling in the atmosphere around you. The entrance of time outside of time into time moves reality from what it was to what it will be in the imaginal realm.

Like your spring bursts forth, and birds dancing in the air catch your eye; the newly leafing trees amaze you with their burst of growth; and you drink in the return of color to a drab world—such is the way miracles move reality from what was to what will be. Do not doubt that there are miracles occurring because you cannot see them. You do see them. You see them in the birds dancing and the leaves bursting and the sun's rising and the green that glows in the sun's reflection, and in these pages that have grown with you in this eight month period so similar to those you experienced when writing A Course of Love.

We have chronicled "the awaiting" and moved now into the time of acceptance of the revelation that has come and come in a new way. "Here" we move from what was revealed, into the awareness that the revelation has occurred. The revelation has occurred. It is real. The new time has come to be and can be chosen ... now.

M

Your brother spoke of a time of acceptance, explicitly bound to time:

"This is a time of convergence, intersection, and pass-through of the finite and the infinite, of time and no time. Time has not yet ceased to be, but as you are in a state of transformation, so too is it. Again, I remind you, as within, so without. As you let go of time's hold on you, it will let go of you. Time will seem to expand but will actually be contracting into nothingness. Time is replaced by presence, by your ability to exist in the here and now in acceptance and without fear."[64]

You were asked to realize that you were being supported, and this you never could see. While your physical life remained outside of the realm of support, you could not fully commit as you have now, due to my direct reassurance.

Do you realize the time in which you now stand?

With no physical change, you have gone beyond uncertainty.

This is what the feminine does! The feminine, unlike even the power of Yeshua, is the power of reassurance, the admission from your counterparts in the borderland, that there will be wine at your wedding! You breathe easier, knowing that you have an advocate who recognizes the needs of form in what appears to be a new way, but is a way as old as time itself.

The masculine energy is so connected to the bigger picture that it does not see when reassurance is needed.

Your Jesus always touched your heart in the particular relationship that you shared. He revealed much to you that you are

---

64 See ACOL D:Day 7.7

only coming to realize. I have also suggested that what may be true by way of recognition, is that your incredible role in the unfolding of The New may not be realized until after your death. Both, I want to tell you, dear one, were what you expected to hear.

Like your Mary Love, I want to surprise you. I desire to delight you. Now I have and I will continue to do so!

You see, it was always as Yeshua said it was—always about acceptance—an acceptance you were not willing to offer until now. This is the beauty of the time being "here," now ... your readiness for it! Your readiness to accept with grace. You are, only now, realizing the nature of what we are about, and that it is really, and truly, creation of The New.

You are realizing it because you have been surprised! Sometimes there is need to be surprised in a personally pleasing way. It is what mothers, sisters and friends all do ... when the time is right.

You are ripe now, and the world is ripe for the coming of The New and its abundance.

Thank you for surprising me, Holy One!

M

Support of The New

Dear Holy One,

I have returned to you after a conference that kept me away for several weeks. My greatest desire on getting home was to hear from you, and you were so kind to surprise me! Thank you. I then had an article deadline to meet and many responses to the conference still await. I hope you will help me now to understand the way forward.

M

In the midst of settling in, I was called to read Days 6 and 7 of "The Dialogues." It was like reading them again for the first time and I have already forgotten what they said, although their impact on me was great. My "sense" of what they said was to accept a new reality. I feel that with your help I am doing this, but I am ... hovering. I *am* between worlds. One is represented by the conference and deadlines, and the other is this one I share with you. Is there really a way to join them, or is it impossible or ... unnecessary?

It is in Day 7 that Jesus said, "Life is now supported." When you gave your promise of support, I didn't remember that Jesus had also offered. Still ... it didn't feel the same.

Jesus then says, "If for no other reason, begin to accept this support of form because it makes sense. It is logical. And realize further that love is not opposed to logic but returns true reason to the mind and heart."[65]

It blows me away to see this ... and to see it, to have been drawn to it, as you are speaking of support! And next Jesus begins to speak of the different relationship that now exists between us and time. I imagine that I will begin to witness, more and more, the complementarity of these ways the two of you bring to me, and us. Many will begin to see the essential vision and its inclusion of form and time.

Yes, sweet one, many will begin to have greater vision.

Yet "here," you have returned from the conference with the vestiges of the abrupt shift in atmosphere if was for you. This, I suggest, is an "others orientation." It is a wonderful time to bring light to this topic of "others" again, as it is delaying many.

I have given you a sense that "others" will support you, but this would not be my preferred way of having you see this, for it then transfers to yourself, and to your relationships that are focused on support of "others." This is not optimal, even while the provision that you desire to offer is good.

My espousal of you, my reassurance, is necessary. It is necessary because you have endured much, because your gift is needed, and because it is the "naturalness" of giving and receiving as one that I call upon.

What you and I are doing is setting the foundation of The New without any bricks. "We" are aligning the internal foundation. You do not need to do more, and I do not want to leave you with the impression that more is asked. No, Mari. Just plain

---

65 See D:Day 7.5

"no." Now it is time to bask in the reception of our Words and the return that will naturally arise from them.

"Naturalness" is the way of The New. The feminine ones understand this, and the feminine is returning. You may even begin to envision the feminine as the acceptance of all that is natural, and a rejection of all that is unnatural. It is very akin to "accept the new, deny the old," but the tone of it is different . . . literally. The words of the feminine are heard in a refreshing way. You leave each of our dialogues altered.

The feminine speak in the language of relatedness. Even the same word, such as "support," delivered from a feminine voice, is different in meaning than the word "support" delivered from a masculine voice.

I am not saying that your brother has not combined the masculine and the feminine in himself, but that in speaking to you as Jesus "the man," which you were and remain encouraged to acknowledge in fact and relationship, there was a "tone" of authority that was heard, and that was, to many, still necessary.

Do you begin to understand? It will take the non-authoritarian feminine voice to break the attachment to authority.

That the voice of the feminine is non-authoritarian does not mean it does not have power. The feminine is the power of giving life. Feminine power is the power of birthing out of one's own being. Birthing new life. The feminine is literally being pushed—squeezed by the twin forces of time and eternity, into predominance—to birth new life. This is also the wonder of Mirari: New Life.

Birth is the most sensate of all events, that without which there would be no universe and no babe to raise to the heavens. The ultimate act of creation is New Life. The feminine "sacrifice" makes sacred through this essential "act"—giving over one's own body and being, to the creation of The New. Your brother, having done this same "Act" in a different way, has birthed this vital Act into the masculine form, where it is but awaiting discovery in His holy way.

This is staggering. I feel myself teetering on the brink of The New.

This is what we are doing: bringing in The New. Both the feminine and the masculine are inclining themselves to the incubating life of The New.

Women remain the womb of the new "here." But it is also the soft strength of our tone that is regenerating life. Our tone both calms the waters and releases the flow. We reverberate. We resound and reflect. We echo the birth of Yeshua in the birth of The New.

M

Eachness Replaces Thingness

We are giving. We are not giving away. I give myself over to you. You give yourself over to me. We give and receive one to another. To give and receive is never to give away. This is crucial to realize as you conceive of wholeness. Your own most intense feelings have arisen over this unusual and off-putting inner knowing that you can never separate from these words to which you gave yourself. You knew to give and hold close, and you fought for your knowing in ways that challenged "the way things are done," the "known wisdom," the way of the masculine-dominated culture.

All the while, you, yourself, never fully understood this. You were accused of thinking you were special. Of unfair expectations. Of egoistic notions about yourself. All of which hurt you greatly as you sought for the reasoning with which you could help those who did not understand—to understand.

This is what we do now, together, as we replace "thingness" and welcome "eachness."[66] *What you can do now is possible because you have received your absolution for the defense you mounted. It has been said that the truth needs no defense. But my Mari, in the world, in this time, sometimes the truth "does" need defense.*

The position in which you found yourself caused you to feel mis-

---

[66] "*Eachness* replaces *thingness* but not oneness." C:20.39

understood and even a little crazy. You were asked, even by friends, "Why does anyone else need to understand?"

Why couldn't you give up when it could not be made clear?

Oh, my dear one, legions of women, and men too, understand—legions of artists—legions of those who have given over their hearts to love. These are already there, and just waiting to be accepted into a new way that does not ask for what they cannot give, and that does ask for what "only" she or he can give.

Admit now that you felt some of our dialogue may need to be deleted, as you struggled with this issue we now bring to light as an essential aspect of wholeness—to give and to hold close! We speak of "giving while holding close" to bring the way of devotion to light. We speak of it to release bitterness. We speak of it to bring change and to create an environment hospitable to The New. We do not speak of it to divide, to make enemies or friends, to villainize or sanitize. We speak of it for the sake of wholeness. For the recognition of distinction. For the coming to know of what is one's own and acceptance of feelings of possession that have been forcefully denied.

This is the meaning of the embrace—the possession, the ownership of belonging—of carrying, or holding relationship and union within one's own Self.[67]

To those who can accept this new way, there will come a time of mourning for the way in which they participated in division of love from love, and you will treat these kindly and with acceptance of the fact that they "did not know."

---

67 See ACOL Dialogues, Day 38

To "know not what you do" is a truth of the time of illusion.

In this new time, the nature—the naturalness—of giving without giving away, will extend. The extension of naturalness will bring those who have always "known," but felt sad or mad or crazy, a calm release. Bitterness will give way to comprehension of the absolute sacredness of being unwilling to sell their soul. In this time in the life of soul, the soul of life is being revealed.

You can recall the words you heard early in A Course of Love that spoke of "the harsh realities" that may "claim your body and your time," and the piece of yourself that "you have set aside" and not allowed it to claim. This is the piece held in your heart, what you will never let life take away from you. "It is the cry that says, 'I will not sell my soul.'"[68]

In your "non-acceptance" of the old, those who do not know they are residing there will begin to realize that they are only a step away, an easily taken step away, from renewing themselves. They will begin to sense that their delivery is at hand. And when it has occurred, they will become tremendous advocates of The New. There will be no shame or blame but only the peace and liberation of new knowing.

---

68 See ACOL C:7.5-6

evival

Early in the days of A Course of Love *you heard that* A Course of Love *would create a new renaissance. This is that of which we begin to speak, and that of which we have been speaking since we began. We speak of renaissance, of rebirth.*

First, I wish to bring to your remembrance the period known by this name. Over three centuries, "revival" changed the world, moving it out of one era (the medieval) to another (the modern). This is literally what we are facilitating—and have been since A Course of Love *first came to you—a new epoch.*

The scale of change was great then and will be far greater now. The pace of change has quickened, along with the pace of time itself, which has been hurtling through this change that is its own rebirth. The joining of the duad of time and time outside of time, will unite a more spacious humanity in creation of The New.

I bring up "a new renaissance" because of the "life on the ground" experiences that are speaking to you, at times seeming to thwart you and at times to compel you. Your life is an example life in this way, in a way of experiencing in advance of most, in advance of realization, the new reality.

Yes, I can believe this, my Mother, and it is very odd. It is often like two feelings in opposition—being propelled and halted. Feeling tremendous energy and inspiration *and* depletion or exhaustion.

That is a good description, my Mari. The irascible nature of time is that it appears to move both slowly and quickly. An hour of time as well as time divided into twenty-four-hour periods of sleep and waking, time given over to birthdays and holidays, to work and vacation, to birthing and aging. Time moves in many ways at the same "time."

As you look back on your life you see the changes that have come. You remember a youth when mothers stayed home and dads went to work, when you knew no one who was divorced, when you sat down as a family for dinner, and "dressed" for church. Life often felt relaxed, slow, at times even dull or constrictive.

You remember how you started your work life on a typewriter, and what a short time ago it was that you had a stationary telephone sitting in your kitchen. Now such lives as were lived then are nearly nonexistent. There are many more single parents and as many divorces. Moms and dads both work. There is the constant "availability" that comes of computers and cell phones as necessity.

You see the slow and fast of time and change. Each of you lives with this daily in fact and memory. Retrospection is needed to see the speed. Circumspection to see the slowness. Introspection to see the removal.

As you wrote a decade ago in Creation of the New, "What matters absolutely is the absolute."

M

The renewal has begun. This is the rebirth, the renascence, the beginning again. This is a making fresh, a giving of spiritual strength, an extension of vision. Like with the renaissance of old, it will be led not by titans of industry, by theorists, or spiritualists, or leaders of countries, but by creatives.

You are called to be creatives for The New.

Lack of vision of the absolute is the removal. Lack of regard for the soul is the reduction. Both are the same.

Led by people who do not know who they are, those who "do" know who they are, are removed. Politically this is life-threatening. Artistically this is soul threatening. In this time, on this planet, it is a global threat. As is always the case, the extreme breeds the balance, and the greatest extreme brings The New.

As in the renaissance of old, the change is of creation.

ℳ

Creation of The New begins as an adaptation of order and design. This has begun. You are in the midst of it. We are throwing open the windows to let in the new air. We, of the way of the Marys, are refreshing that which has grown stale, that which thinks it knows what to do, that which clings to the way it has been done, that which would "use" The New in ways of old. Your brother spoke at length of "use" for this reason.[69] In letting go what was known of the ways of old, the order and design is naturally new and of the new time. This causes indignation, but is not, yet, seen as a threat. In this way, The New is quietly taking hold, and the opening for The New is constantly being expanded. Time outside of time is intruding, penetrating the old. The world "is" being refreshed. You "are" being renewed.

In each one's "personal life" the rejuvenation is at hand. As each one takes their stand for soul, the movement begins to spread.

ℳ

---

69 See ACOL C:Chapter 29.

The Quickened

The days when you are forsaken and, in your forsakenness, find your way as "your life," are the days when you are no longer of the Father, the creator of all. These are the days I've described as being of the Mother, creator of one. Both the masculine and feminine are capable of giving over their lives to birth them newly. This is the time in which you now stand. The new renaissance. The New Advent. The great departure, and the great arrival. This is happening in each "one," by which I mean in each heart that hears the call to The New and follows it in her or his way.

The way is open.

The quickening has begun.

M

It is those who have given room to their grief who are ready to navigate this birth, for the end of the old will feel like a separation from many, including wives from husbands and children from their parents. Those caught in the old will become great challenges for those who are moving on. The feeling will be mutual, but those of the old will have solid reasoning in their favor, and solid facts on the ground on which they stand. "This is the way it is."

The forsaking of all "others" will be the way as you move into the realm of no "others." No "others" means that all are one with you, and you will begin to realize that your allegiance to The New will not affect one here and one there, but all.

You will, of necessity, give up on the old way, for to try to live in both realms will make you feel insane. When Yeshua cried out, "Eli, Eli, lema sabachthani?" "My God, my God, why have you forsaken me," he was quite human in his suffering, in his grief, in his experience of the insanity of the time. More and more around you will begin to experience the feeling of unreality, if not insanity, and you will at times be put off balance by this. You will feel sorrow for needless suffering, including your own, for you will feel as if you "suffer" this change: some of you often, some of you seldom, all of you at one time or another.

ℳ

But suffering is healing.

This suffering makes you aware of the actuality, the necessity, of the change that is the dawning reality of one realm. One realm is that which is coming into existence. The new time begins to merge with you, even before it becomes a reality for all life on Earth. This is what you, my beloved, felt within your womb. This merging. This quickening. This new life. It is all related.

You will see that each experience of your life has joined with you and made you whole, and that you are a microcosm, a miniature universe, being enlarged and spreading, elongating time until it snaps back and becomes a whisper in the wind. A time of no time, or spaciousness, breezes in . . . populated by wonders of the imaginal realm.

What calls you and what creates for you will be imagination

itself. You will see for yourself, as you reside in the imagination of the divine duad, that you will create in this same image and in a contiguous way. This is the way of Mary. You will bypass the way of old and anchor "the New within the web of reality."[70]

The conception of the duad brings forth this new creation.

Out of the duad of God the Father and God the Mother came creation. Out of the duad of yourself and Jesus came A Course of Love. *In the duad of you and me, we bring forth* Mirari: The Way of the Marys. *Do you begin to understand?*

"Those called to the way of Mary are called to be what they want to see reflected in the world and to the realization that this reflection is the new way of creation. In their being they become what they want to create."[71]

Finishing out Day 18, your Jesus asked you to show, to demonstrate, your feelings and said that these feelings "are the creations unique to you."

The quickened are in and within this time of "showing their feelings." They are transparent in their demonstration of this human face of love, which is what they have chosen, and been chosen by their nature, to be. They do this in relationship, which is the only means by which feelings are shown.

In A Course of Love, *it was stated that, "Mary represents the relationship that occurs within, Jesus the relationship that occurs with the world. So do each of you."*[72] *Your brother was conveying*

---

70 See ACOL Days 17 and 18 of The Dialogues

71 ACOL D:Day19.4

72 ACOL D:Day18.2

that, while many will experience and live both ways, one or the other will, from their own nature, regardless of maleness or femaleness, be primary—yet not separate from the other. The ways will exist in union.

This movement is the movement of the quickened, the new life emerging from the personalized duad of Being in time and eternity.

M

To Forsake All Others

My Mother, I am experiencing some stress. Just in saying that, I begin to realize the reason. It is so silly that I didn't realize it before. There has been "stress" because a vulnerable person in my life has been in crisis and checked into the hospital. It has become "distress" because I have stayed out of the drama of it as much as I've been able, more than I ever have. I have not rushed to the rescue. It was time, I felt, in our relationship, to behave in this way. But it was disconcerting.

Rather than continuing to receive from you while I was in that mood, I had this idea to view some old writing from the time in which my initial attempt at "rescue" was falling apart. I got involved in it. This was in the early days after *A Course of Love*, and the time just after the cabin was first completed. These were not calm days. Often, the cabin offered the only solace I could find.

Jesus continued to talk to me, as you know, and he said many lovely things, like my being "the birth mother" of our Course, things that coincide with what you say, but I was still so lost, externally, in normal human life and its struggles, so desperately trying to navigate it and get rid of it at the same time.

On finally having the time and space I longed for, I began to unravel, with Jesus' help, all the confusion that this, along with A Course of Love's lack of success, had generated.

I feel that these two situations have been making me introspective and a little sad, and that it is no accident. The sense of abandonment . . . that I am abandoning, or at least not rescuing someone I love . . . is jarring. Yet, all these things came up in a haphazard way that I know is not essentially haphazard.

Oh, my daughter, the word, "abandon" is so perfect. Do you know its meaning? It is to give up, completely, and forever, or to give over, completely and forever. It is very near to the meaning of "forsake." To "forsake" all "others," which is, in many ways, what your early call to receive Jesus was, and what the time of the cabin was about.

It was about forsaking "others" . . . to answer a greater call.

While you loved this work, your desire to be known as who you are, as your Self, was also true and deep and heartfelt. In not being known, you were nursing a broken heart. For years you did this without realizing what you were doing. You were still trying to figure things out, and only through having this recur and recur, and fail, and fail, and fail, were you brought to those days when your brother told you that you had to quit. Without that time, which was only the beginning of this long path you have walked, you would not be where you are now. You are now in the new time of release to the freedom, love, joy, and mutual recognition of the "truly real" that you desire. This is what you always desired.

The word "recognition" was a culprit of many of your wounds. You were wanting to be known in the fullness of who you are, and "recognition" was taken by many, (including yourself at times), to be a longing for a title, a public, or as a greater contributor to A Course of Love *than you were thought to be. You were treated as if you wanted special status, when "specialness" was as like unto sin as anything in a newly "sinless" way of thinking.*

In this way, you were demeaned.

What has been new of late is that you have not accepted being demeaned. Due to this, it became the right time for you to receive and be invited into our way of Mary. If you can fully accept this, you can be such a light to your sisters and brothers! All have been unrecognized and demeaned in the time that is passing. Most do not see that this is the cause of their broken hearts or see cause for rejoicing that their hearts have been broken open to what can now be released: waves of love and freedom from the demeaning.

Strangely, the word "demeanor" is the nearly perfect opposite from the trial of the demeaned. It is to govern oneself, and to lead in that way, by the example of one who is not governed by unnatural forces, including "others."

M

There was a day when Yeshua called you to be radical for love. This made you so happy. I called you to be radical years ago and do so again. You are called, as are all moving into the way of Mary, to radically live out your relationship to the spirit of love. By being a radical, as Yeshua was, you are going to the roots of your human nature and the Cause of your divine nature.

"Radical," as well as the similar "radicle," "radix" and "radius," are like unto the straight-line Jesus spoke of. He used, as an example, a needle passing through the layers of an onion.[73] Your brother spoke of this similarly when he brought you the unknown word "monistic" in these words:

"The person who knows, truly knows, the simplest truth of the identity of the Self no longer lives in a dualistic position with God,

---

73 See ACOL C:22.5

but in a monistic state with Him. The difference is in realizing relationship with the infinite instead of the finite, with life as opposed to matter."[74]

When you are undivided in your Self, you know that you and your Source are One, and are then able to accept the coupling of the duad. The duad is unity with Source experienced in relationship. It is union with all the beloved companions of the physical world, as well as with non-physical beings. The Self is always primary as the knower, the source of joining with trees and stars ... and time. When you know the Self, life begins again, and life continues to begin again with each new awareness, awareness of all that abides with you in the relationship of union.

This is a perfect example of knowings you held but did not "know." You did not know of what you knew. You knew in the way of the scientist. You had a "sense," a sense of a mystery, and you followed your nose, your instincts, but without the scientific need to prove that which was sensed. And truly now, I want you to see, that although you railed about needing to be understood, you knew that, in this new way of knowing, you did not need to "understand." What could be more radical?

Still, how delighted you were many years later when this meaning of the word "monistic" was revealed (in part by a diagram of a circle with a dot in its middle)![75] The reality of one whole with no "separate" parts is revealed as the true reality. This, we combine now, with the reality of the duad that always exists—that of the knower and the known: two as one and one as two, neither separate.

---

74 ACOL C:30.7

75 A diagram first revealed to me by ACOL reader, Steve Huck.

There are so many meanings in all this that they could make your head spin!

But not as many as in A Course in Miracles, *as Jesus, in his second course,* A Course of Love, *was beginning to speak of the wholeness of what had once been divided into parts. In response to your naturally arising quest for wholeness, he began to reveal a common ground on which seemingly disparate parts of self could meet. All suggested the point of encounter—one and another—in the "union" of sharing in relationship.*

Now, you and I have brought forth the duad ... the two together.

What is "between" one and another, and where the world intersects with you, speak of the same phenomenon. Both speak of mystery, and the call that cannot be answered with thought alone, but only with joining. We speak of what has been hidden in plain sight: The mystery itself.

Here, you and I share the beauty of the mystery!

The beauty of the mystery is that it goes before you always. This is the divine secret, the "super" natural. Mystery is all that is beyond human "understanding." Do you see? Mystery is all that is beyond the "knowledge" of the thinking mind. Those initiated into "the mystery" did not learn some bit of knowledge. They became aware of how to live without it. They became aware of the mystery that would go before them unto the end of time.

The mystery of creation.

Mystery speaks its own language, a language that becomes the expression of one's inspiration, the prose of one's faith, the text of one person's own conviction, repentance, new life ... and the sharing of it.

A New Advent can only extend into a New Pentecost: communication between God and persons in New Acts. These are the acts that create wholeness while not obliterating union and relationship. It is "here," in this time, that the duad of Heaven and Earth will enter such relationship as will "act upon" the fabric of time and eternity, human and divine unity.

M

Prelude to Our Way of Mary: Acts

On this day, when you are feeling low, even "mortified" for making a small mistake and for not expressing enough gratitude, I hope to comfort and inspire you, and all of those who are entering The Way of the Marys, and who will do so imperfectly, and with vestiges of the old nipping at your heels.

You will be told that you are "in your head" by those who wish to use the way that is passing against you. You will be told by others that you are "not using your head." You will be told that you are ungrateful at just such a time as when you may be called to be exactly that—ungrateful toward those who continue in the way that is passing. You may be called illogical, egoic and, as you have seen, the "swear" words of those who would use ideas such as "specialness" for their own aims by suggesting that you think you are special.

Yes, there is care to be taken here, and a respect for those who are still lost, as well as for those of the way of Jesus. You may be able to see that many of those who are of the way of Jesus are still growing into their realization that their way is concluding, even while still necessary. They must now balance the ways that supported the former time with the ways that will support the new time. As you know, this is not easy.

Many will begin to understand the role of the "example life." They will no longer teach the old but will clarify the call to the new. They may do this even as they transform into, or support, the way of Mary.

Many more will be tempted to resist, but temptation can be a helpmate to the realization that the temptation comes of clinging to the old—and that these too, are called to embrace The New. Those who can carry on with helpful acts in time will actually support Acts outside of time. These will be appreciated for their contributions.

An "act" is a thing done, a deed, a doing. An act is a thing of movement. Your reception of these words is an Act of giving and receiving as one. Without the Act that takes place "in time," there would be no movement, being, and expression toward the astonishment and wonder, the Mirari, of The New.

M

Rest

Before going forward to the new Acts of movement, being and expression, in this time of Mirari, you are invited to take a breath and rest in the spirit of love.

Together, we put the old to bed as we would a small child in our care. We kneel beside the bed in prayer. We kiss the forehead of what is passing as we would an elder on the way to being once again a youngster. We believe in miracles and put our faith in love. We rest in gentleness as we are prepared to be radical forerunners of The New.

Do whatever grieving is still needed for the way that is passing, for we are completing the life that existed in the time that is passing. Recognize that it has served you well and delivered you to The New.

Here is where timidity is set aside for the courage at the heart of wholeness. Here is where the mighty "one" embraces as the trembling two, the power called upon to give and receive The New.

In this time of unity, dedicate all thought to unity, as all thought is made over in the way of love that will birth Mirari: The Way of the Marys, and the way of The New.

Benediction For The Reader

Feel my grace upon you as this breaking open occurs for you and all your sisters and brothers. There is a place beyond the idea that there is "sense to be had" or sense to be "made" from what occurs. A place beyond and within. The boundaries you have held are fading. There is a crack in time and space. The New comes to you as your own heart bids it come.

Your embrace, like mine, makes holy. I thank you for continuing to care for life. Now accept that care which extends from Mari and me. Through your embrace, new life comes to the ones who have passed and the ones who remain, to the way that has passed, and the new way coming to be.

Let your embrace of events turn inward to find a resting place from which your feelings and your passion find acceptance "from you." Begin to extend outward with that power with which you will create "your new," The New that reflects ... You. Hear your heart's protest, its outcry, its passion as well as its compassion. Be propelled by the energy of The New, knowing ... always knowing ... that in love, in life conceived by love, all are welcomed home to love.

~ Mary of Nazareth

M

End Note

JUNE 2020

As I was finishing the needed introduction, which is always one of the final pieces written, my husband Donny was burning the last of the spring brush in preparation for new planting. What a strange, miracle-like coincidence of timing!

This is right where the vision that begins "Mirari" occurred, and the flames are now real. The scent of woodsmoke fills the air and my senses. Sparks, and bits of ash flit up from the fire like rare birds. What is in my sight joins the image that started it all seven years ago. I marvel at the mystery of it, my own certainty amidst uncertainty, the wonder of the masculine in Donny, other cherished men in my life, and the ascent of the feminine. I see the feminine rising as surely as I see the fire petals that are soaring off like waves of changing form.

I know it is the masculine in me that has driven me to manifest, and I mourn that this energy is now waning.

I remember balance.

It is difficult for any of us to fully achieve a balance of our roles, change our patterns, or voice our truths. I, myself, am very averse to conflict, which has not meant I do not enter it, only that I rarely resolve it. But as my friend Christina Strutt recently suggested, "You speak it no matter whether anyone hears it or not."

That's our part. To speak it.

On June 4, when I completed the final manuscript, I did not realize that June the 4th is the hundredth anniversary of the women's right to vote passing Congress. Only one hundred years ago! For many of us, our mothers or grandmothers were among the first generation of women to have this right, to be equal citizens. That has never seemed more mind blowing than it does today.

It was less than sixty years ago that the Civil Rights Act was signed into law (July 2, 1964), and (as I'm on my final review prior to publishing) the LGBTQ have just gained the same rights (June 15, 2020)!

I realize, as I conclude, that much of this writing is a lament. Maybe the lament: allowed, heard, acknowledged, is the final piece.

Maybe we should all get together and lament!

This movement into the new isn't only like grief, it is like a divorce. You always leave something behind. Maybe you have to lament before you can trust in what awaits. And then there arises a ridiculous, giddy feeling.

I have begun to trust that I am cared for. And with that, I can care enough to look out for "myself" as well as our movement into The New. I can remind myself and you that "self-love" often comes last.

I can also see that you and I may feel the most irritation about the "way things are" just before we are ready to leave the old behind. One affair needs to end before a new celebration can come. It is a new day. The New is ahead of you, and you can afford to be kind. You can see the past in a new light and be thankful that you can do so. You can even reunite for weddings ... or supply the wine!

Each of us can let go ... when the time is right. It is part of this grand movement to The New.

To you, and all, I offer hope that answers to our prayers will rise out of the fire of the new; that as the flames reach skyward, they bring you the uncommon thought, the unnamed inspiration, and the self-love that allows you to find your voice, share it with a friend (or the world), and in this way, "be" the spark ... be among the many dazzling lights that are igniting The New.

"We" are the changing form of the world.

Mari Perron, June 15, 2020

M

ostscript

BY CHRISTIE LORD

On June 5, 2020, the day after Mari completed the final draft of "Mirari," I (Christie Lord, a long-time friend of Mari's) had an amazing conversation with my partner, Pamela, who is currently a resident at a Minneapolis nursing home. Because of the COVID-19 pandemic, our meetings are restricted to "window visits." I stare at her through a window two stories above my head. She looks out at me below, where I stand in the facility parking lot. Pam uses a staff cell phone and I bring my phone from home. Generally, these phone calls are less than satisfying since Pam's memory is sporadic and she often finds it hard to retrieve her words. However, this particular Sunday afternoon was extraordinary.

I was rambling on about the pandemic, the strain of "social-distancing," and the George Floyd protests on Lake Street, (near our home) when Pamela suddenly interrupted: "There was another important thing that happened yesterday," (June 4, 2020), she stated matter-of-factly.

"Oh, what was that?" I responded.

"The Second Incarnation," she answered.

After a moment I asked, "You mean the incarnation of the feminine face of God or something like that? (I had never heard Pam use the word "Incarnation.")

"Yes," Pam replied. "Tell Mari."

"I will," I said, and I did! Mari and I smiled with a sort of gleeful knowing when I told her of Pam's announcement. "This is indeed the Way of Mirari, the Way of Wonder," we laughed.

Thank you, Pamela!

M

Answers to my Prayers and Gratitude for my People

First—Mary of Nazareth.

I will never be the same. She has changed me, and I adore her.

Mother Mary has been charming, stunning, and compassionate, along with radical, revolutionary, and wise. Yet what I am particularly grateful for is her support of women and of me. Yes, mainly she is inclusive of the feminine leaning man too, and ultimately of all, but for much of the book she is saying it is time, not only for the Divine Feminine, but for women to take up their power.

Let us safeguard this right for ourselves and all.

I would guess there are a lot of us who appreciate Holy Mary's offer of "support." I don't particularly like the word "support," even though she uses it in just the right way. It might be that I haven't favored the word because of all those times I did not get support when I needed it. (Don't get me going on the staggering amount of child "support" that never gets collected. You cannot tell me the government can hound you for the $500 in taxes you owe and just can't find all those men who owe in aggregate, over 100 *billion* dollars in unpaid child support.)

The continuing failure to reach Gender Pay Equity—equal pay for equal work, exasperates the situation.

Having been a "poor" single parent for a while, and at other times a lower middle-class married mother, and in situations in other areas of life as well, (worker, business owner, writer), I know that women can come, after a while, to feel we must be so strong that we no longer need support; that "support" makes us weak; even that it is undeserved.

That is such a load of hooey.

Holy Mary also speaks of "suffering" in this book, and I want to give you a definition of suffering (albeit a partial definition) that I found right within my old Webster dictionary, and ask you to remember its connection to suffrage and suffragettes:

Suffer: to undergo, endure, experience (any process, esp. change) Especially change.

Change does not come easy. But it is occurring—it will come. *It will come.* And in this "new" time, it will come . . . creatively. Because of Holy Mary I feel enlivened enough to invite you to give yourself the freedom to be a creator of The New. Give yourself the freedom to be in dialogue. Give yourself the freedom to accept support and to support others.

The most gladdening thing (to me) is that Holy Mary offers her radical encouragement that women *Rise to their holy place in life*, and the way she substantiates my, and I think many women's, complaints about the "way things are." She upholds our warranted vision of how they could be.

I am thankful that she is continuing her support. Our next book explores the themes of "new" Acts, Revelations, and Testaments of The New. A third book will follow.

Thank you to my Beloved Jesus who joined us once in a while, and who knew, as always, just when I needed him.

I offer so much appreciation to my friends who offered such generosity in both reading and offering many suggestions along the way to getting *Mirari: The Way of the Marys* into readiness for you.

Mirari: The Way of the Marys / 347

To Christie Lord and Christina Strutt, (my staunchest and longest running supporters,) "You saved me from myself, and saved *Mirari* from being long delayed. Thank you with all my heart."

An equally heartfelt thank you to my friend Terry Widner for designing the graceful cover story with the heart of the craftsman that he is, and for continuing, even under circumstances that were not ideal.

I offer thanks to Kate Macnamara, who "experienced" a bit of the "experience" with me on occasion (invaluable), and to those who read and repeated Holy Mary's beautiful words back to me: Lady Burke and Rhetta Morgan.

Lee Flynn is the first man to read or speak these words. Hearing Holy Mary's words, read in his sonorous male voice touched me, as did comments from my "writer friend" Michael Mark. Michael stunned me with his expression of the ways in which "Mirari" moved him. Maybe for that reason, he agreed to do a round of edits with me! The "editors" became like my eyes and ears and each deserve an "Oh, my God, thank you!"

I knew I needed these sensitive, ACOL-reading eyes. Susan Lister Bernardini offered her time and talent, and just as I thought I might never get through it, two local (St. Paul, Minnesota) women, Debra Ricci and Pamela Laughing Waters answered my call for help. They were the midwives at the birth. Debra had graciously donated her time for a first-round edit, and along with Pamela, rescued me when I was floundering with the final. Besides the editing, Debra made me a beautiful lunch and Pamela ran the manuscript back and forth between us!

Finally, Danny Neese also offered support and perhaps elicited from me my first unqualified, "Yes, please."

You can always hope you have the funds to hire services, but the blessings that come of collaboration, at least "after" the work is done, could not be more full of the wonder of Mirari!

I am forever thankful to my family, who always stretch my heart, and to Mary Love who is "like family" and expands my heart's knowing in a different way! Mary also took the cover photograph.

Writing in this way is like flying without a safety net. You have all delivered me to a safe landing.

I am appreciative of the local talent at Wise Ink who provided publishing expertise, for the interior design by Patrick Maloney, who formed a beautiful "whole" from the voices of Mary, Jesus, and me, and the expertise combined with kindness that Graham Warnken provided in the production phase.

Finally, thank you to all of *A Course of Love*'s readers and supporters who have embraced this way of love and shared with me their anticipation for the way of Mary being further developed, as it has been, in *Mirari: The Way of the Marys*.

Being moved and being able to "move" even one other person with words, is a privilege. It is a joy and a power many of us can call upon in creation of The New.

I invite you to accept our gift of the wonder of Mirari, to become radical creatives for The New, and to create only Love.

M

Referencing Guide

References to quotes from *A Course of Love*:

The Course (C)
The Treatises (T) (as there are four Treatises, they are related as: T1, T2, T3, and T4
The Dialogues (D) (as there are both Chapters and Days, you will see: D:1 as well as D:Day1
The references follow book, chapter, and verse.
Example: C:2.1 signifies The Course, chapter 2, verse 1
You will find this same order in regard to the other books of A Course of Love's Combined Volume: T1:2.1, T2:2.1, T3:2.1, T4:2.1
Dialogue chapters as D:2.1 and Dialogue Days as D:Day2.1

A Course of Love is available from online retailers or at https://acourseoflove.com

RELATED WORKS

The Given Self: Recovering Your True Nature, Mari Perron (2009): This highly personal yet universal exploration, moves toward wholeness through one's own humanity and embrace of the authentic self.

Creation of the New, by Mari Perron (2007): A mystical experience with relevance to this new work, from a place of thinking without thought. Mystical language and imagery, announces "the new."

The Grace Trilogy, (1997)
Love, by Mari Perron, Julieanne Carver, and Mary Kathryn Love; Grace, by Mary Kathryn Love; Peace, by Mari Perron; The books: Love and Peace, share the story of the experiences of three close friends who "felt into" new ways of being together and sharing their profound experiences with each other and with angels. "Grace" is a personal, profound, and tender experience of grief and new life. Each of these books are being reintroduced by Course of Love Publications.

ONLINE RESOURCES

https://www.wayofmary.com
Mariperron.com https://www.mariperron.com

You can find me on video by searching Mari Perron on YouTube.
https://www.youtube.com/user/perronmari/videos

SHARING

I hope you will take up the call, spread the word, and connect. Share "Mirari" with your friends. Post some of Holy Mary's beautiful quotes. Make room for the new babe and the gentle rising of liberation that Holy Mary calls you to.
See the Way of Mary website for selected quotes and referencing.
https://www.wayofmary.com

SUPPORT THE SHARING

The "Center for A Course of Love" holds the copyright and Trademark for *A Course of Love*. It is a stationary site (not one added to often) but it speaks for not "oldening" the work and emphasizes letting it propel us into The New.

https://www.centerforacourseoflove.org/

The Center offers two search engines. One, Discover ACOL, will be helpful for those who would like to easily find any of the quotes from *A Course of Love* that are referenced in *Mirari: The Way of the Marys*. https://www.centerforacourseoflove.org/discover-acol/

The Center, and Mari Perron, gratefully accept your gifts. https://www.centerforacourseoflove.org/ways-to-give/

M

www.ingramcontent.com/pod-product-compliance
Lightning Source LLC
Chambersburg PA
CBHW032025290426
44110CB00012B/681